On Second Language Learner Acquisition of English Collocations

James Martin Rogers
Meijo University, Japan

Series in Education

Copyright © 2024 Vernon Press, an imprint of Vernon Art and Science Inc, on behalf of the author.

All rights reserved. No part of this publication may be reproduced, stored in a retrieval system, or transmitted in any form or by any means, electronic, mechanical, photocopying, recording, or otherwise, without the prior permission of Vernon Art and Science Inc.

www.vernonpress.com

In the Americas:
Vernon Press
1000 N West Street, Suite 1200
Wilmington, Delaware, 19801
United States

In the rest of the world:
Vernon Press
C/Sancti Espiritu 17,
Malaga, 29006
Spain

Series in Education

Library of Congress Control Number: 2023947657

ISBN: 978-1-64889-943-0

Also available: 978-1-64889-797-9 [Hardback]; 978-1-64889-826-6 [PDF, E-Book]

Cover design by Vernon Press. Cover image by James Martin Rogers.

The supplementary material can be downloaded from https://vernonpress.com/book/1877

Product and company names mentioned in this work are the trademarks of their respective owners. While every care has been taken in preparing this work, neither the authors nor Vernon Art and Science Inc. may be held responsible for any loss or damage caused or alleged to be caused directly or indirectly by the information contained in it.

Every effort has been made to trace all copyright holders, but if any have been inadvertently overlooked the publisher will be pleased to include any necessary credits in any subsequent reprint or edition.

For my daughter

Table of Contents

	List of Figures and Tables	vii
	Preface	xi
	Acknowledgments	xiii
Chapter 1	**Introduction**	1
Chapter 2	**Review of the Literature**	5

    Introduction
    Overview of Second Language Learning Research
    On Learners' Lack of Collocational Fluency
    On the Learning Burden of Collocations
    On Approaching and Defining Collocations
        What is a Collocation?
        Types vs. Lemmas vs. Word Families
        On Semantic Transparency
        On Concgramming, MWU Length, and Colligation
    On the Value of Collocations
    On the Lack of Research and Resources
    On the Direct Teaching of Collocations
    On Utilizing Corpus Data to Identify Collocations
    On Using L1-L2 Congruency to Identify Useful Collocations
    Conclusion

Chapter 3	**Addressing Gaps in the Research**	37

    Introduction
    The Gaps in the Research

Research Methods and Techniques
> Research Paradigm
>
> Data Source, Collection Methodology, and Analysis

Filling the Gaps in the Research
> What is an Ideal Corpus Frequency Data Cut-off for Identifying High-frequency General English MWUs?
>
> Is Corpus Dispersion Data Reliable for Identifying High-frequency General English MWUs?
>
> Is Corpus Chronological Data Reliable for Identifying High-frequency General English MWUs?
>
> Is Consideration for Colligation an Important Criterion for Identifying High-frequency General English MWUs?
>
> What Percentage of High-frequency General English MWUs is Deemed by Fluent Speakers Worthy of Expanding Beyond Their Most Frequent Exemplar?
>
> What Percentage of MWUs Most Representative of High-frequency General English Lemmatized Concgrams Has Low Semantic Transparency?
>
> What Percentage of MWUs Most Representative of High frequency General English Lemmatized Concgrams Has Low L1-L2 Congruency With Japanese, Chinese, and Korean?
>
> Is Fluent Speaker Intuition Reliable Regarding High-frequency Vocabulary Usage in Context Creation?
>
> What is Japanese University Students' Knowledge of MWUs Most Representative of High-frequency General English Lemmatized Concgrams?

Conclusion

Chapter 4	**Implications and Applications**	87
Chapter 5	**Conclusion**	101
	References	105
	Index	115

List of Figures and Tables

List of Figures

Figure 3.1.	Percentage of Items Accurately and Erroneously Flagged for Balanced Dispersion Data Distribution at All Three Parameters	48
Figure 3.2.	Total Items Erroneously Flagged or Judged Unbalanced Which Were Not Flagged	48
Figure 3.3.	Percentage of Items Accurately and Erroneously Flagged for Balanced Chronological Data Distribution at all Three Parameters	55

List of Tables

Table 2.1.	The Three Approaches' Ability to Identify Common Collocates of the Verb 'Play'	13
Table 2.2.	High-frequency Collocations for the Four Most Frequent Words in the Word Family for 'Govern' According to the COCA (Top Frequencies in Bold)	16
Table 2.3.	A Sample of Data From the COCA for a Concgram Search for the Lemmas 'Provide' and 'Support'	19
Table 2.4.	Top Three MWUs for the Lemmas 'Provide' and 'Support' Found After Examining 500 Concordance Strings in the COCA	20
Table 2.5.	MWUs Identified From 500 Example Sentences in Which the Lemmas 'Come' and 'Term' Both Occur in	21
Table 2.6.	A Comparison Between Two MWU Searches, One With and One Without Consideration for a Specific Type of Colligation	22
Table 3.1.	Word Frequency Breakdown of Lemma Pairs Occurring Once Per Million Tokens According to Vocabprofile's 25,000-word Families of the BNC and COCA	44
Table 3.2.	Criteria for Rating the Value of Collocates for Learners of General English	47
Table 3.3.	Items Found Not to be Worthy of Inclusion Because They Were Either Inappropriate Language, Grammatical Formulations, Duplicates, or Compound Nouns	49

Table 3.4.	Samples of Items Flagged for Having Unbalanced Dispersion in Each of the Four Most Common Genres at All Three Parameters	49
Table 3.5.	A Sample of Pairs Flagged for Having Unbalanced Dispersion at All Three Parameters Judged to be Erroneously Flagged by a Fluent Speaker	51
Table 3.6.	A Sample of Pairs Judged to be of Little Use to General Learners Not Flagged for Having Unbalanced Dispersion by Any of the Three Parameters	52
Table 3.7.	Samples of Items Accurately Flagged at All Three Parameters (2.5, 5, and 10) and Items Judged to Have Chronological Issues Not Flagged by Any of the Parameters (X)	56
Table 3.8.	The Top MWU Identified When 500 and 1,000 Example Sentences Were Utilized	59
Table 3.9.	Amount of Top MWUs That Were Affected by Each of the Colligational Treatments	61
Table 3.10.	Comparison Between Ten Random Samples of Top MWUs Affected by the Colligational Treatment for Pre-nominal Possessive Pronouns and the Results That Would Have Occurred Without the Treatment	62
Table 3.11.	Comparison Between Ten Samples of Top MWUs Affected by the Colligational Treatment for Subject Pronouns and the Results That Would Have Occurred Without the Treatment	63
Table 3.12.	Comparison Between Ten Random Samples of Top MWUs Affected by the Colligational Treatment for Cardinal Numbers and the Results That Would Have Occurred Without the Treatment	64
Table 3.13.	MWUs Identified From 500 Example Sentences in Which the Lemma Pair 'Come' and 'Term' Both Occur	67
Table 3.14.	Semantic Transparency Ratings of the Collocations (Percentage of Total Items in Parenthesis)	69
Table 3.15.	L1-L2 Congruency Ratings of High-frequency English MWUs With Japanese Translations	71
Table 3.16.	L1-L2 Congruency Ratings of High-frequency English MWUs With Chinese Translations	71
Table 3.17.	L1-L2 Congruency Ratings of High-frequency English MWUs With Korean Translations	72
Table 3.18.	Word Family Frequency Breakdown of Formulaic Phrases Using RANGE	74

Table 3.19.	Word Family Frequency Breakdown of Formulaic Phrases Within Example Sentences Created Using Fluent Speaker Intuition Using RANGE	75
Table 3.20.	Vocabprofiler Breakdown of Top 3,000 Word Family Words Not Covered by Example Sentences Created Using Fluent Speaker Intuition	77
Table 3.21.	L1-L2 Congruency Ratings of MWUs Selected for Testing Students' Collocational Fluency	79
Table 3.22.	Mean Scores for Test Items Organized by Frequency Level	81
Table 3.23.	Multiple Regression Analysis and Correlation Coefficient with TOEFL as the Dependent Variable and Item Frequency as the Independent Variable	81
Table 3.24.	Multiple Regression Analysis and Correlation Coefficient with TOEFL Score as the Dependent Variable and L1-L2 Congruency as the Independent Variable	82
Table 4.1.	Top Ten TOEIC Gains in Comparison to Minutes Studied with the App	98

Preface

Gaining control of collocations is a very important part of language learning, but learners are typically slow in sounding native-like in their use of collocations. One of the reasons for this is that the majority of collocations occur infrequently. It is useful to bear in mind that the frequency of any collocation will be lower than the frequency of its lowest-frequency member.

Collocations have the chance of being learned across the four strands of a well-balanced course. In the meaning-focused input strand of a course, collocations will be met through listening and reading. Because learning through the strand of meaning-focused input is largely incidental learning, large quantities of input through extensive reading and extensive listening are needed to get enough repetitions of particular collocations for them to stay in memory. Collocations also have the chance to be learned through meaning-focused output, that is, through speaking and writing, where learners have the opportunity to turn receptive knowledge into productive use and to strengthen and enrich their knowledge of collocations. The fluency development strand is likely to be a very important strand in the development of collocational knowledge as the pressure to use language faster encourages a focus on restructuring knowledge to achieve fluency by moving from the processing of single words to greater use of multiword units. These three meaning-focused strands all depend on incidental learning and frequency of occurrence.

The strand of language-focused learning provides the opportunity to speed up the learning of collocations through deliberate teaching and deliberate learning. Such deliberate teaching and learning are most efficiently done if there are well-researched lists of collocations to draw on. This book reports on research that has been done with this goal in mind.

The case for giving deliberate attention to collocations is strengthened by research that suggests that, as with the deliberate learning of vocabulary, the deliberate learning of collocations simultaneously results in both implicit knowledge and explicit knowledge. That is, the deliberate learning of collocations will provide the kind of knowledge that is needed for normal language use.

In order for something to be learned, there are three requirements of attention. Firstly, what needs to be learned needs to be focused on. That is, the form, the meaning, and/or the use of the collocation needs to be focused on. Secondly, there needs to be a quantity of attention. In other words, there needs to be repeated encounters and good attention for each encounter. The greater the amount of attention, the more likely the collocation is to be remembered. Thirdly, there needs to be good quality attention. In the case of collocation, the quality of attention can be increased by looking at how the parts of the collocation relate to the meaning of the whole, the use of the collocation in a variety of contexts, and visualizing the meaning of the collocation. These requirements of attention apply to both incidental and deliberate learning. In incidental learning, the three requirements are typically not as strongly applied as in deliberate learning. In incidental learning of collocations, as in listening and reading, there tends to be brief attention to the form, with similarly brief meaning recall. Each incidental meeting tends to involve a small amount of attention, but with repeated meetings, there can be a cumulative effect. The quality of attention is typically not very deep, involving a brief focus on the form and contextual meaning.

The research in this book provides very useful support for the deliberate learning of collocations. It makes sure that, in deliberate learning, attention is focused on the most useful items to learn.

Paul Nation

Acknowledgments

I would like to thank all research assistants and translators who volunteered their time for my research projects in the past. Without their help, I wouldn't have been able to tackle the large-scale research projects this book will describe. Filling the gaps in the research would have also been difficult to accomplish if not for the software solution that was provided by Dr. Laurence Anthony.

Chapter 1

Introduction

Collocations are words that have a high frequency of co-occurrence, and researchers agree that collocational fluency is an extremely important part of second language acquisition. However, there is evidence that students struggle to obtain such knowledge and that there is a lack of focus on developing it in the classroom. This lack of focus is connected to a lack of comprehensive and reliable resources that identify which items to focus on. This chapter will thus highlight the various barriers that prevent students from obtaining collocational fluency. By becoming cognizant of these issues, it will then be clear to readers why answering gaps in the research regarding collocations is crucial to improving the efficacy of second language acquisition.

In recent years, more and more researchers are beginning to recognize the value of collocations for second language learners. Lewis (2000a) stated, "Teaching collocation should be a top priority in every language course" (p. 8). This view stems from the realization that much of the language we speak consists of prefabricated chunks and that collocation is one of the most important kinds of chunks. Hoey (2005) and Hill (2000) also agreed that collocations play a central role in language. So, what does this central role of collocation encompass for the second language learner? Multiple researchers cited how competent use of formulaic language helps language learners sound more natural (Durrant & Schmitt, 2009; Cowie, 1998; Wray, 2002). In addition to aiding learners in making more native-like selections, the use of collocation has been shown to make for more efficient language processing (de Glopper, 2002; Nation, 2001).

However, despite teachers being aware of the importance of collocations, their students still struggle to obtain collocational fluency (DeCock et al., 1998; Kallkvist, 1998; Waller, 1993). Research indicates that students (even advanced ones) struggle with collocations, and this is a major barrier to obtaining complete fluency in a second language. For instance, Laufer and Waldman (2011) found that three separate proficiency levels of Hebrew students studying English all produced far fewer collocations than native speakers and that even though the number of collocations increased at the advanced level, errors persisted. Nesselhauf (2005) examined a 150,000 token learner corpus written by advanced German learners of English and found that a quarter of the 2,000 verb-noun collocations found were wrong and a third deviant.

So why is it that students lack collocational knowledge? Despite being aware of collocational fluency's importance, there is a severe lack of emphasis on teaching collocations. Nesselhauf's (2005) study found that the number of years learners were taught English had no positive effect on collocational knowledge. Furthermore, textbooks may not be giving students enough repetition in regard to collocation. Gitsaki's (1996) examination of a junior high school ESL textbook series found that there was very little recycling of collocations across the three books. The arbitrary nature of criteria for selecting useful collocations to teach also contributes to the problem. The Japanese Ministry of Education (Monbukagakusho, 2003) simply stated one of the goals of secondary English education is that basic collocations should be chosen for instruction, but gave no further guidelines as to which should be taught and has not updated this guideline since then.

Furthermore, should collocation instruction be informed by grammatical matrices, as Mitchell (1971) and Gitsaki (1996) suggested, or can we limit the amount to focus on by using frequency data, grammatical well-formedness, L1 congruency, and semantic transparency, as Shin (2006) did? With Shin's approach, not only frequently co-occurring collocations are identified, but collocations with a higher learning burden than others (collocations with either low L1 congruency or semantically opaque) are also. Or does the sheer number of collocations rule out any methodical approach to teaching, as Mackin (1978) claimed? If collocations are defined by frequent co-occurrence, how should we count such lexical co-occurrence? Should lexis be counted as word types, as Shin (2006) did, or would word families or lemmas be ideal? Are positional variation and constituent variation (concgramming) important criteria to consider? If so, can currently available concordance software process data in a way that will help identify items most worthy of study? What would be an appropriate frequency cut-off for high-frequency collocations, and do the resulting identified items constitute a practical learning goal for direct study? These and several other important questions remain unanswered.

If teachers and materials writers are aware of the importance of collocational fluency, why not focus on them? The reason is a severe lack of reliable resources to refer to in selecting collocations worth studying directly. Furthermore, a reliable methodology for identifying such collocations still does not exist; thus, many questions remain. Regarding currently available resources to help learners acquire collocational fluency, small-scale collocation lists do currently exist, and a small number of large-scale lists as well (albeit with flawed methodologies). So, no large-scale lists utilizing modern methodologies that organize items by frequency and L1-L2 congruency for item selection existed until I filled this major gap with my research. The following chapter will provide the basis for answering the questions above and many other important questions by giving a detailed review of the current literature and providing evidence of a major gap in the research.

Chapter 2

Review of the Literature

Introduction

Collocational knowledge is a part of second language acquisition that learners must master, but what exactly is a collocation? In fact, collocations are quite challenging to define and identify. This literature review will discuss the various ways collocations have been defined and identified and each methodology's virtues and limitations. This chapter will also discuss what previous research says about the value of collocational knowledge and the lack of collocational knowledge among learners throughout the globe. Previous research on the learning burden of collocations, the lack of research and resources, the large amounts of data that must be grappled with, criteria to use to identify collocations, and the direct teaching of collocations will also be discussed.

This chapter will cover all pertinent research areas to improve second language learners' collocational fluency. The main goal of this literature review is to highlight research that defines or clarifies the phenomena of collocation, points out the importance of collocational fluency, identifies a lack of knowledge of collocations, and points out how resources that help develop second language learners' collocational fluency are limited. It will also review research that has utilized corpus data to help identify valuable collocations and research that specifies essential criteria to consider when identifying useful collocations, such as L1-L2 congruency.

This literature review will only briefly examine theories related to native speaker acquisition of collocational knowledge because my research thus far has focused on creating materials that would help ESL learners obtain collocational fluency. Such learners acquire collocational fluency in very different ways due to the practical limitations of exposure, and therefore, comparing their acquisition of collocations to that of native speakers is not appropriate. This review will also only touch upon studies concerned with how collocations are stored in the brain because my previous research had the practical pedagogical intention of identifying high-frequency collocations to teach directly to ESL students. This literature review will also not delve into differences in collocations among the varieties of English for several reasons. First, since parts of my research required native speaker judgments on language, reliable judgments cannot be made for a variety of English that is not one's mother tongue. Second, age and quality issues regarding certain corpora led me to work with data from only one specific corpus, which consists of American English data.

Overview of Second Language Learning Research

How does a person achieve fluency in a second language? Ellis (1985) stated that theories on second language acquisition abound, that perhaps there are too many, and that some may have been accepted as fact too soon. Hadley (2001) discussed these theories by placing them on a continuum, with empiricists on one side and rationalists on the other. Empiricist theories of language learning include Skinner (1957), who proposed that 'operant conditioning' is how learning occurs in humans. Positive and negative reinforcement by the community shapes the language a learner will use. From this theory's viewpoint, the human mind is a tabula rasa upon which pre-established accepted language patterns are imprinted. Rationalist theories, such as Chomsky's (1957) 'universal grammar,' rejected such empiricist theories by insisting that humans are innately programmed to learn language.

In more recent years, other theories have been developed. Gasser's (1990) connectionist theory of language acquisition would fall close to Skinner's on the empiricist end of the continuum. It describes language storage in the brain as a network of interconnected units that are "strengthened or weakened in response to regularities in input patterns" (Gasser, 1990, p. 179). On the other end would be Krashen's (1982) 'monitor model,' which stated that conscious acquisition of grammar rules occurs when a person learns a language, along with unconscious acquisition.

However, despite the contradictions between such theories, Larsen-Freeman and Long (1991) suggested that accepting only one of these theories as omnipotent at this early stage in language acquisition research would not be prudent. This is true today as well. For instance, despite much research on language acquisition, there is still disagreement regarding a universal language acquisition theory. Many researchers still argue about the shortcomings of the theories mentioned above. Furthermore, new shortcomings are still being identified. For example, Lewis' (1993) 'lexical method' theorized that collocation, not grammar, may be the overarching organizer of language.

Considering that my research focused on the identification of high-frequency collocations, which constitutes a major gap in the research, it is clear that Larsen-Freeman and Long (1991) were correct in suggesting that it would be imprudent at this stage to assume that any one theory should be accepted. Many questions remain unanswered in this field, even some of the most important fundamental questions, such as a general language acquisition theory. Moreover, there is no consensus on defining a collocation, let alone identifying the common ones in English. Since Lewis (1993) suggested that the linguistic phenomena of collocations may be the central language organizer, more research is clearly still needed, even today.

My research thus far aimed to take a step toward developing a methodology that will define and identify the common collocations of English and the formulaic language they most frequently occur in to improve upon the efficacy of second language acquisition. These findings can not only be used to inform pedagogy but also to help researchers further develop overarching theories of language acquisition.

On Learners' Lack of Collocational Fluency

Learners having problems with collocations is a well-established fact (Biskup, 1992; Bahns & Eldaw, 1993; Howath, 1996; Granger, 1998; Nesselhauf, 2005). Even as early as the 1970s, researchers wrote about learners lacking this essential aspect of language knowledge. Researchers such as Grucza and Jaruzelska (1978), Marton (1977), and Arabski (1979) all note that a large percentage of student errors are collocational in nature.

A lack of collocational fluency among second-language learners is also a universal issue. Research shows that learners from various backgrounds struggle to obtain collocational knowledge. In Europe, second language learners struggle. Bartan (2019) noted that 47% of Turkish learners' verb + noun collocation errors were due to L1 influence. Peters (2019) found that Dutch learners struggled more with incongruent collocations than congruent ones. Linnarud (1986) found that Swedish learners utilized collocations much less than native speakers. Biskup (1992) found that Polish and German university students lack collocational fluency. Bahns and Eldaw (1993) found that approximately 50% of collocational phrase translations by German EFL students were incorrect. Nesselhauf (2003; 2005) also showed that German students struggle with collocations. Jaen (2007) showed that university students studying English linguistics from Spain also had poor collocational knowledge. In the Middle East, second language learners struggle as well. Keshavarz and Salimi (2007) found that Iranian EFL learners also have insufficient knowledge of English collocations. Davoudi and Behshad (2015) found that collocational errors rooted in L1 influence among Iranian learners accounted for 75% of the errors in essay writing. Fayez-Hussein (1990) found that Jordanian university students majoring in English could not provide the correct answer approximately 50% of the time when their collocational knowledge was tested. Asian learners struggle as well. Both Lin et al. (2003) and Liu and Shaw (2001) found Taiwanese university students to have limited collocational knowledge. Tseng's (2002) questionnaire even revealed that Taiwanese high school students knew little of the concept of collocation.

Rogers (2013) found collocational fluency among the weakest vocabulary depth knowledge that Japanese university students possess. Zhou (2016) found that Chinese learners tend to overuse certain high-frequency words when attempting to make collocations incorrectly.

For some time, we have known that collocational errors make up a considerable percentage of second language learner errors in general (Korosadowicz-Struzynska, 1980). Furthermore, this is not just a problem for lower-level students. In fact, we have also known for some time now that even advanced-level learners struggle with collocational knowledge (Brown, 1974; Channell, 1981; Cowie, 1978; Hausmann, 1984; Mackin, 1978; Rudzka et al., 1981). Unfortunately, the problem persists. In the 1990s, Bahns and Eldaw (1993), Biskup (1992), Gitsaki (1996), and Kjellmer (1990) all noted that high-level learners have limited collocational fluency. More recently, Liu and Shaw (2001), Wang (2001), and Nesselhauf (2005) also found that advanced learners continue to lack collocational fluency. But what makes collocational fluency so challenging to acquire?

On the Learning Burden of Collocations

Obtaining collocational fluency is not an easy task to accomplish. Researchers have been cognizant of the difficulty of mastering collocational fluency for some time. Wilkins (1972) stated that "the appropriateness of idiom to situation is very difficult to master" (p. 128). Similar opinions continue to this day. The sheer number of collocations that exist poses a barrier to obtaining fluency in them and doing collocational research. Among the research done so far, Kjellmer's (1987) study was the most comprehensive, examining the co-occurrence of lexis as low as two occurrences per million tokens. However, many collocations deemed useful by native speaker intuition occur much less frequently than twice per million tokens. For example, items occurring as low as once per hundred thousand tokens can be considered worthy of teaching, such as the following lemma pairs: 'nice/vacation,' 'finish/workout,' and 'tend/exaggerate' (Davies, 2008).

Both Hill (2000) and Pawley and Syder (1983) believed that the number of 'lexicalized sentence stems' that native speakers have at their disposal is in the hundreds of thousands. Sinclair's (1995) COBUILD English Collocations list has 140,000 different collocations. Bahns (1993) gave a lower estimate, in the tens of thousands, but still referred to this as an obstacle. Hill (2000), while admitting that estimates vary, remarked that "70% of everything we say, hear, read, or write is to be found in some form of fixed expression" (p. 53). He stated that we need to accept that the learning load to become fluent in a second language is not 40,000 items but closer to 400,000 or more. Other researchers agree, pointing out that Nation's (1990) previous estimate of undergraduate native speakers' vocabulary sizes of 20,000 items may be misleading since this only constitutes "the rudimentary base of the native speaker's lexicon" (Conzett, 2000, p. 75). Therefore, the quantity of collocations is a challenge for the learner. In addition, regarding why there is a lack of a particular kind of collocational research (specifically identifying 'useful' collocations), the large number of items to examine is a barrier. There are simply so many collocations that it is difficult for one or even a team of researchers to handle.

While it is difficult to pinpoint precisely how many collocations a native speaker has in their lexicon, some researchers have estimated the number to be in the hundreds of thousands (Hill, 2000). For instance, Davies' (2010) collocation list had 50 collocations with the lemma 'water' having more than 500 occurrences per 425 million tokens, and while the value of the higher frequency collocations, such as 'drink' and 'water' (3,099 occurrences), is clear, even collocations with much lower frequencies, such as 'splash' and 'water' (592 occurrences) have apparent value. Gitsaki (1996) agreed, stating that "one of the main reasons the learner finds listening or reading difficult is not because of the density of new words, but the density of unrecognized collocations" (p. 54).

Hill et al. (2000) highlighted another issue that makes obtaining collocational fluency difficult: its complexity. They state:

> Collocation is never as simple as it seems - sometimes the adverb must come in front of the verb, sometimes it must come after, and sometimes either position is possible with very similar meanings. Some adjective + noun or verb + noun combinations are much more common if they are used in the negative; perhaps some of the verbs are used with the headword mostly when it is literal, others mostly when it is more metaphorical. Very rarely are the lines between two 'different' uses of this kind clear. (p. 116)

Learners struggle with this complexity and often make errors by overgeneralizing or substituting a generic term for something usually represented by a more specific term. For example, the word 'tool' would be used instead of the word 'pliers.' Fayez-Hussein (1990) found that such errors accounted for 38.3% of the collocational errors made in his study.

Another issue that Moon (1997) noted is that the non-compositional nature of how collocations are formed necessitates that learners recognize, learn, decode, and encode them as holistic units, which significantly adds to their learning burden. The results of Jaen's (2007) study on collocational knowledge of university students in Spain also showed that the arbitrary nature of how collocations are formed is problematic and responsible for the students' difficulties with them. Laufer (1990) also made a point to mention this issue, referring to it as the "rulelessness of collocations" (p. 147). Fayez-Hussien (1990) gave the example of 'several thanks' versus 'many thanks' and learners' inability to use logic to determine why one is appropriate and the other is not.

Furthermore, how semantically bonded a collocation is also affects its learning burden. Nesselhauf (2003) found that the highest error rate occurred with collocations with a medium degree of restriction. Keshavarz and Salimi (2007) stated that Iranian students struggled with restricted collocations. Howarth (1996), Huang (2001), and Nesselhauf (2003) noted a similar weak point in that, in their studies, learners tended to make errors with restricted or semi-restricted collocations. Biskup (1992) found the same issue. In his study, Polish students only produced acceptable restricted collocations correctly 22.6% of the time, while German students only produced them correctly 16.6%. Liu and Shaw (2001) found this issue as well. In their study, learners produced significantly fewer free combinations than prefabricated units.

Learners also seem to struggle with particular types of collocations. Hsu and Chiu (2008) found that the learners in their study never produced adverb/ adjective collocations and recommended that teachers focus on such items. Liu (1999) found verb-noun errors to be the most common collocational error that Chinese college students made. Liu's (2002) study revealed that 87% of errors Taiwanese students made were verb-noun combinations, and in 93% of them, the verb was the problem. Moon (1997) found phrasal verbs to be problematic for learners. Nesselhauf (2005) discovered that specific semantic groups of verbs were difficult for her students. Her German students particularly struggled with the verbs 'achieve,' 'reach,' 'acquire,' 'obtain,' and 'gain.' In general, many researchers also cite a collocation's semantic transparency as affecting its learning burden. Gitsaki (1996) cited semantically opaque examples, such as 'foot the bill' and 'high explosive,' and their obvious potential to mislead. Therefore, whether an item is semantically transparent and whether students know this can affect a collocation's learning burden.

Durrant and Schmitt (2009) highlighted a variety of research that shows that learners tend to overuse certain collocations, especially if they are frequent, neutral, or exist as a cognate in their L1. As mentioned above, L1-L2 congruency, or how similar/dissimilar a collocation's translation is in the learner's native tongue, significantly influences their learning burden. Gitsaki (1996) highlights how "In English people 'draw conclusions' while the Greeks 'bga;zounsumpera;smata' [take out conclusions]" (p. 3-4). Fayez-Hussein (1990) gave the example of how students produced 'pipe water' instead of 'tap water.' Both Nesselhauf (2005) and Fayez-Hussein (1990) found that approximately 50% of collocational errors were due to L1 influence, and thus, such items should receive more teaching time. Chan and Liou (2005) noted that 38% of collocational errors were due to L1 influence. Chen (2002) found L1 interference to be a common source of errors by Taiwanese high school students. Because these researchers, along with Al-Zahrani (1998), Bahns (1993), and Biskup (1992), are all aware of the affect incongruency has on a collocation's learning burden, they all called for increased emphasis on such items.

Patterns of underuse and overuse of certain collocations have also been noted by DeCock et al. (1998), Granger (1998), Lesniewska and Witalisz (2007), and Lorenz (1999). Durrant and Schmitt's (2009) study also showed that learners significantly underuse collocations with a mutual information (MI) score of over seven. They also found that learners do not use as many low-frequency collocations as native speakers.

These studies highlight why obtainment of collocational fluency is a difficult task. Specifically, they highlight how particular types of collocations have a higher learning burden than others, such as arbitrarily bonded collocations, restricted collocations, L1-L2 incongruent collocations, and low-frequency collocations, among others.

However, although the studies mentioned in this and the previous section make it quite clear that second language learners across the globe struggle to obtain collocational fluency in English and, in particular, have difficulty with certain types of collocations, previous research has yet to comprehensively pinpoint the extent to which aspects of collocational fluency cause difficulty for learners. My research aimed to fill this gap in the research by judging in fine detail Japanese university students' general collocational knowledge and whether certain aspects of collocations, such as frequency, semantic transparency, and L1-L2 congruency, play a factor in increasing a collocation's learning burden.

On Approaching and Defining Collocations

What is a Collocation?

One of the issues of contention in many of the studies conducted on collocations is a lack of consensus on defining what a collocation is. Cowan (1989) and Shin (2006) stated that there is too much variability in researchers' definitions of the term. For instance, many researchers defined collocations by their tendency to frequently co-occur (Firth, 1957; Hoey, 1991; Jones and Sinclair, 1974). Others used syntactic structures (Gitsaki, 1996; Zhang, 1993). Some researchers even used a combination of frequency data and syntactic patterning to identify collocations (Lesniewska & Witalisz, 2007).

The three main approaches to researching collocations must first be discussed to understand the merits and demerits of these valid methods of defining collocations. The three main approaches to studying collocations are semantic, structural, and lexical. In the semantic approach, collocations are defined as being predictable by their semantic features (Robins, 1967). This approach explains why particular lexical items occurred only with certain others. However, Gitsaki (1996) pointed out that a weakness of this approach is that there is "a large number of idiosyncratic co-occurrences or combinations that are arbitrarily restricted…they are left unexplained and marginal by semanticists" (p. 35). Gitsaki (1996) listed some examples, such as how 'kick the bucket' and 'blond hair' can only be used when referring to humans (p. 33). Lewis (2000b) agreed that trying to use semantics to explain why certain words co-occur leads to, at best, "half-truths" (p. 13).

Meanwhile, the structural approach utilizes grammatical patterns to explain collocation, and proponents believe that collocation is influenced by structure. Mitchell (1971) proposed that collocation be studied within these "grammatical matrices" (p. 48). Gitsaki (1996) agreed since her study of 275 Greek learners of English at three separate proficiency levels showed that the learners did not once use some particular collocation patterns, such as adverb/adjective collocations, and that these were avoided due to their structural and syntactic complexity and relative infrequency in English.

Halliday and Sinclair (1966) began considering lexis separate but complementary to grammatical theory. They believe it is necessary to consider collocation's influence on the organization of language because grammar alone is not enough to determine which lexical item would occur due to the idiosyncratic nature of collocations. Halliday (1966) cited how word choice can also be specified by collocational restrictions in addition to structural and semantic limitations (p. 152). He gave the example of how 'strong' is a member of a lexical set with 'tea,' and 'powerful' is a member of a lexical set with 'car' and not vice-versa, which cannot be explained by the structural or semantic approaches. Lewis (1993) stated that language "consists of grammaticalized lexis, not lexicalized grammar" (p. vi). The lexical approach thus views lexis, not grammar, as the overarching engine that organizes language. Hill (2000) agreed, distancing himself from "previously cherished structuralist ideas" (p. 48) and noted that instead of breaking down language into smaller and smaller categories, we should try to view language in the largest units possible.

However, a study focusing on lexical collocations may contain the kind of grammatical collocations that Durrant (2009) stated are important. In fact, Rogers et al. (2021) showed that a study of a significant enough scale could identify both, as the grammatical collocations Durrant (2009) identified existed within the larger collocations Rogers et al. (2021) identified. This approach may thus be ideal for particular research goals in that it strikes a balance between providing learners with both types of collocations and coincides with Halliday and Sinclair's (1966) complementary relationship between lexis and grammar.

Each of these approaches has its strengths and weaknesses, and their usage depends on the type of research being conducted. However, the lexical approach has advantages over the semantic and structural approaches, as shown in Table 2.1 below. The verb 'play' actually has many different meanings in English, and the examples below highlight them. The most typical usage people will think of is its usage to describe participation in a game or sport or the use of a musical instrument. However, one can also 'play politics' or 'play a character' in a film. 'Politics,' 'character,' 'sports,' and 'musical instrument' are all nouns, so the structural approach would identify the pattern 'play' + [noun]. However, we can also say 'play himself/herself/yourself/themselves,' thus, the structural approach would miss all instances of 'play + [pronoun].'

Table 2.1. The Three Approaches' Ability to Identify Common Collocates of the Verb 'Play'

Collocates of the verb 'play'	Semantic Approach	Structural Approach	Lexical Approach
play [sports] / [instruments] / [music] / [games]	O	O	O
play politics / play a character	X	O	O
play himself/herself/yourself/themselves	X	X	X

The semantic approach also fails to cover all usage of the verb 'play.' The semantic approach uses logic to understand the verb's usage. You 'play' something you need to practice, such as a musical instrument, a sport, or a character. However, the logic of this approach fails with 'play politics' and 'play himself/herself/yourself/themselves.'

However, the lexical approach can identify all of the above-mentioned co-occurring patterns by only focusing on the frequency of co-occurrence. Although each approach has its place in collocation research, the above examples highlight the significant advantages of the lexical approach for the goal of particular types of research, such as the types of research I intended to conduct to fill gaps in the literature to improve upon the efficacy of learning collocations by second language learners.

Therefore, a lexical approach was taken in my research to ensure that all important collocates are identified. I defined collocations in the traditional sense as words with a high frequency of co-occurrence (Biber et al., 1999; Shin, 2006). My approach also included some aspects of a structural approach, and the justification for this will be discussed later in this book. However, before beginning this research, it was still unclear how the criterion of frequency should be applied since previous research does not indicate a frequency cut-off that should be utilized to identify high-frequency collocations worthy of direct study.

Types vs. Lemmas vs. Word Families

Word combinations such as 'jury's verdict' are identified when we define collocations by their tendency to co-occur frequently. However, combinations such as 'of the' are also identified. Should such grammatical combinations also be considered 'collocations'? Does teaching 'of the' have value to a second language learner? Shin (2006) believed that it does not, explaining that an essential criterion of collocation identification is that it needs to be a meaningful unit, or in other words, grammatically well-formed. One way of accomplishing this is by only considering content words as collocations (nouns, verbs, adjectives, and adverbs), as Shina and Woolard (2000) did. Ackermann and Chen (2013) also similarly limited their dataset by only examining verb-noun, adjective-noun, adverb-adjective, and adverb-verb formulations. My research also took this approach by only considering nouns, verbs, adjectives, or adverbs collocations while allowing for grammatical words such as 'of' and 'the' to occur before, after, or between the collocations.

It is also important to further explore the definition of collocations. For example, Biber et al. (1999) deemed collocations to be two-word phrases that co-occur, distinguishing them from idioms and lexical bundles. With second language learners in mind, this is not ideal. Take, for instance, the collocates 'crux' and 'matter.' These two words collocate, but never simply as a two-word phrase. They always collocate within the larger chunk 'crux of the matter.' Therefore, limiting the definition of collocation to two-word phrases excludes items that clearly collocate. Researchers such as Conzett (2000) improved the definition of collocations by considering two or more frequently co-occurring words as collocations, or what is more commonly referred to as multi-word units (MWUs).

Defining MWUs is problematic as well. A variety of terms have been used to describe them, such as 'phrase patterns and sentence patterns' (Twaddell 1973), 'combinations of lexical items' (Korosadowicz-Struzynska 1980), 'conventionalized language forms' (Yorio, 1980), 'word associations' (Murphy, 1983), 'fixed expressions' (Alexander 1984; Kennedy, 1990), 'prefabricated language chunks and routinized formulas' (Nattinger & DeCarrico, 1992), and 'formulaic language' (Wray, 2002). Categorizing different types of collocation is also problematic because they often overlap in their description. Therefore, my research explored this in detail and created new methodologies to identify MWUs that consist of a pivot word and a collocate that frequently co-occur.

Furthermore, there is the issue of how words should be counted. Should they be counted as word types, as Shin (2006) did? With his word-counting approach, all words with distinct spellings were counted separately with no attempt to consolidate data. This contrasts with counting words as lemmas or word families (more on this distinction below). Such a method would successfully identify the 'crux of the matter.' However, in certain circumstances, this is not an ideal way to count the frequency of co-occurrence. The reason is the number of collocations that exist in a language can be in the hundreds of thousands (Hill, 2000; Pawley & Snyder, 1983), and there is a clear, practical need to consolidate data in some way if the goal is to identify collocations worthy of direct study. My research focused on identifying collocations to teach second language learners directly. Thus, an approach was necessary to deal with the copious amount of collocations that exist. Realistically speaking, there simply is insufficient classroom time to teach every collocation. Fortunately, options are available to help consolidate data, such as by counting words as word families and lemmas.

Word families include "a base word and all its derived and inflected forms" (Bauer and Nation, 1993, p. 11). For example, the word family for 'govern' is represented by the headword 'govern,' which represents 'governed,' 'governing,' 'government,' 'governmental,' 'governments,' 'governor,' 'governors,' 'governorship,' 'governorships,' 'governs,' 'govt,' 'intergovernmental,' 'misgoverned,' 'misgoverning,' 'misgoverns,' and 'ungovernable' (Heatley et al., 2002). In contrast, lemma groups are much less inclusive. A lemma, as defined by Nation and Meara (2002), is a "set of related words consisting of the stem and inflected forms that are all the same part of speech" (p. 36). For example, the verb 'run' would be the lemma representing the verb forms 'runs,' 'running,' and 'ran,' while the noun 'run' would be listed as a separate entry.

There are issues with counting using word families. Webb and Nation (2008) remarked that if learners demonstrate knowledge of a headword, there is an assumption that they also have receptive knowledge of the rest of the word family. However, depending on the study's goal, using word families may not be ideal. For instance, Schmitt and Meara (1997) found that Japanese high school and university students had poor English affix knowledge. Daulton (2008) agreed, stating that it is "imprudent to assume that Japanese learners can extend word knowledge within word families" (p. 120).

Furthermore, if teachers have the practical goal of teaching high-frequency vocabulary, ideally, such vocabulary should be taught along with its high-frequency collocations in the form of MWUs. When a teacher selects a word worthy of teaching using word families, one or more examples must be given. Let us imagine a situation where a teacher needs to teach a word within the word family for 'govern.' By using frequency data from the Corpus of Contemporary American English (COCA) (Davies, 2008) and counting frequency in lemma families, Table 2.2 below shows that the lemmas in the word family which have the highest frequencies are 'government,' 'governor,' 'govern,' and 'governmental.' When relying on native speaker intuition, these four words are of clear value to be taught directly to second language learners. In contrast, other words in the word family are considered to have either marginal or low value for direct teaching. The table also lists those words' most frequent collocations. The corpus data reveals the collocation 'federal government' as the most frequent. However, very different but still valuable collocations also occur with the other lemma in the word family with vastly different frequency counts. So, what should teachers do when presented with the task of teaching one of the words in this family? Should they rely simply on the most frequent collocates in this family? If so, and they provided four examples for the learner, they would all be collocates for 'government,' and all other collocates for the other common lemmas in the word family would be excluded. This data set clearly shows how word families have the potential to be overly inclusive.

Table 2.2. High-frequency Collocations for the Four Most Frequent Words in the Word Family for 'Govern' According to the COCA[1] (Top Frequencies in Bold)

Pivot Word (frequency)	Collocates (frequency)
government (220,945)	**federal (15,542)** local (5,022) officials (4,336) agencies (2,721)
governor (42,639)	former (2,438) Republican (1,322) lieutenant (890) Democratic (750) office (748)
govern (8,552)	rules (721) laws (424) law (250) country (240) regulations (238)
governmental (4,374)	agencies (232) affairs (186) action (115) committee (113) institutions (112)

[1] Excluding proper nouns such as person's names and states.

This data makes it salient that a more practical alternative to types and word families would be to count words using lemmas, which is the procedure that I adopted in my research. For example, consider the lemma pair 'take' and 'walk.' First, should all of the MWUs of the lemma pair 'take' and 'walk' really be counted separately as types? Aren't the MWUs 'take a walk,' 'take walks,' 'took a walk,' and 'taking walks' essentially part of the same group? Practically speaking, considering the copious amount of data I dealt with as I tried to achieve my research goals, the answer is yes. In addition to the advantage of having fewer items to study, counting co-occurrence in such a way leads to more reliable frequency counts. For example, in the COCA (Davies, 2008), the types 'take' and 'walk' have a co-occurrence frequency of 1,125, while the lemma pair 'take' and 'walk' have nearly twice that at 2,049.

Moreover, imagine a learner studies the MWU 'took a walk,' and then later 'take a break.' Would that learner be able to comprehend 'take a walk' without directly learning it? The answer is there is a high probability that they would not have to because the affix knowledge necessary to comprehend the inflections that noun, verb, adjective, and adverb lemmas are comprised of poses a very low learning burden. It is even more apparent when noun lemmas are considered. For example, learners clearly do not need to learn 'powerful engine' and 'powerful engines' at different times. They simply have to master the general rule of how to pluralize nouns in English to have sufficient knowledge to comprehend such items.

On Semantic Transparency

Semantic transparency, or how literal/figurative a collocation/MWU is, has often been utilized to identify collocations. Van der Meer (1998) discussed the distinction between what some refer to as 'free combinations,' or semantically literal formulations, as being different from the category of collocations. Researchers such as Moon (1994; 1997) stated that such literal formulations are not worthy of direct study by second language learners. However, rather than limiting myself to rigid definitions of the term 'collocation,' my research focused on what word formulations are of value to teach second language learners. With such a goal in mind, not including free combinations as collocations becomes problematic because issues such as L1-L2 congruency come into play. Fayez-Hussein (1990) found that 50% of collocational errors were due to L1 interference. Thus, a literal collocation can still pose a high learning burden if it is incongruent with how it is said in the learner's mother tongue. Additionally, I discovered that most high-frequency collocations consist of literal formulations, and by not including them, many high-frequency collocations become ignored.

The learning burden of collocations can be categorized using semantic transparency, such as how Grant and Bauer's (2004) taxonomy broke formulations down into literals, collocations with one non-compositional element (ONCEs), figuratives, and core idioms. With everything relative, semantically opaque collocations such as ONCEs, figuratives, and core idioms pose a higher learning burden than literals. Hence, researchers such as Martinez (2013) suggested a framework that uses semantic opacity in ordering how phrases are taught. However, Macis and Schmitt (2017) noted that the MWUs that most textbooks teach are literal combinations.

Other researchers insist that literal collocations be taught directly for reasons besides the issue of L1-L2 congruency. Nesselhauf (2005) found that students sometimes assign literal meaning to collocations with a figurative meaning and vice-versa. Gitsaki (1996) noted that such collocations even show "a certain degree of syntactic frozenness and resistance to lexical substitution" (p. 49). Therefore, similar to the approach taken by Macis et al. (2021), my research defined collocations without excluding literal formulations since teaching them can be useful for learners. However, where high-frequency MWUs fall on a spectrum of semantic transparency has yet to be comprehensively determined in previous literature. Thus, my research also aimed to fill this gap.

On Concgramming, MWU Length, and Colligation

As discussed earlier, it is clear that it is not ideal to simply count words as types and provide learners with such word sequences to study. Such a method does not result in ranking co-occurrence reliably. Counting the occurrences of collocations does present itself with some issues, such as constituent variation. For instance, researchers such as Renouf and Sinclair (1991) used syntactic frameworks to grapple with discontinuous sequences. Wilks (2005) used a more advanced approach by utilizing skipgram searches, which can handle constituency variation. For example, it could be argued that 'close friends' and 'close childhood friends' should be counted together since it is essentially the same collocation, albeit with an adjective added.

Cheng et al.'s (2006) concgramming method was a significant step forward in that it counted co-occurrence not only with consideration for constituent variation but also positional variation. A concgram, as they defined it, "constitutes all the permutations of constituency and positional variation generated by the association of two or more words" (p. 411). Constituency variation (AB, ACB) involves a pair of words not only co-occurring adjacent to one another ('lose weight') but also with a constituent ('lose some weight'). Positional variation (AB, BA) refers to counting the total occurrences of two or more particular lexical items, including occurrences on either side of each other. So, 'provide you support' and 'support you provide' would be included in the total counts for a MWU concordance search for the lemmas 'provide' and 'support.' They stated that "searches which focus on contiguous collocations present an incomplete picture of the word associations that exist" (p. 431) in that the majority of the collocations they found in their study were non-contiguous, showing both constituency and positional variation. This can be seen in Table 2.3 below, which shows the first four results of a concgram search for the lemmas 'provide' and 'support.' This data is sourced from the COCA's online interface, which allows for lemma concgram searches and provides snippets of the sentences these concgrams occur in.

Table 2.3. A Sample of Data From the COCA for a Concgram Search for the Lemmas 'Provide' and 'Support'

...low-cost measures, the United States can extend the same lifesaving **support** that it has **provided** to the little boy in a rural, dusty village to the working-age woman living...
...it, then provide technical support to assist them. This **support** can usually be **provided** through a single phone call or demonstration. If needed, seek assistance from school...
...losing those aid dollars that we need in order to get **support** when Pakistan does **provide** it, which is real and does help us in the case of drones to...
...for low-income adults in occupational programs as well as financial **support** to colleges to **provide** support services for such students. States and colleges interested in adopting a model similar...

However, simply identifying lemma pairs that co-occur frequently is insufficient to provide learners with specific items to study. For instance, 'take' and 'walk' collocate, but it is not enough to simply expose students to this lemma pair. Instead, a more specific example of how the two words collocate as a MWU needs to be identified. Is the most frequent combination 'taking walks,' 'took walks,' 'take a walk,' etc.? Therefore, steps are required to identify the MWU most representative of that lemmatized concgram. This can be accomplished via concordance software like AntConc (Anthony, 2018). With such software, concordance data from a corpus can be processed to identify the MWU most representative of a lemma pair. When 500 example sentences containing both the lemma 'provide' and 'support' from the COCA were processed with AntConc, it was revealed that 'provide support' is the most common MWU that occurs. Table 2.4 below shows the top three MWUs for this lemma pair.

Table 2.4. Top Three MWUs for the Lemmas 'Provide' and 'Support' Found After Examining 500 Concordance Strings in the COCA

MWU	Frequency
provide support	55
support provided	39
support provided by	32

Concgramming has significant advantages when the goal is to identify MWUs most representative of high-frequency collocations. Attempts to identify MWUs that are not done as concgram searches thus have the potential to be unreliable. Unfortunately, much of the previous research that aimed to identify high-frequency MWUs was conducted without consideration for positional or constituent variation (Biber et al., 2004; Shin, 2006; Simpson & Mendis, 2003). Therefore, there is a clear gap in the literature that my research aimed to fill.

Furthermore, another pertinent question is whether an MWU identified as most representative of a lemmatized concgram should go beyond the pivot and collocate. For instance, should an identification method stop at 'take a walk,' or should it extend beyond this to identify 'take a walk to'? An example of the need for such an approach can be seen in Table 2.5 below. The lemmas 'come' and 'term' co-occur, but as evident in the table, only 'come to terms' is identified as the most frequently occurring phrase in which the two lemmas co-occur in a corpus data search. However, 'come to terms with' occurs nearly as much as 'come to terms' but is not identified as the most frequently occurring. With available concordance software, extending MWUs beyond their pivot and collocate is impossible. Therefore, a fluent speaker must be relied upon to extend the sequence beyond the most frequent MWU to its left or right when the speaker judges any additions as part of the natural unit. This is possible by having fluent speakers rely on their intuition to only add strings to the core formulaic sequence that truly represented common usage, but that also provided learners with helpful information. While somewhat subjective, practically speaking, such a method improves the ability to provide learners with valuable information on how collocations are typically used. However, my later research incorporated corpus frequency data into this judgment to address the subjectivity in such judgments.

Table 2.5. MWUs Identified From 500 Example Sentences in Which the Lemmas 'Come' and 'Term' Both Occur in

MWU	Occurrences in 500 sentences
come to terms	243
come to terms with	229
to come to terms	133
to come to terms with	129
coming to terms	96
coming to terms with the	86
to come to terms with the	44
come to terms with [pre-nominal possessive pronoun]	28
coming to terms with the	26

    There is also the question of how long a MWU should be. In my research, the maximum length of a MWU was seven words long. The rationale for this length stems from findings on typical human memory limitations (Miller, 1956). It is worth noting that some previous research identified collocations without such a limitation. Morley (2015), for example, identified common academic phrases in typical rhetorical patterns, or 'moves.' Although this approach can provide helpful information to learners, some of the items he identified are more than 15 words long and may be too long to be considered phrases. Instead, they function more like exemplar sentences rather than MWUs.

    Colligation, or counting various lexical items that can easily substitute for one another as grammatical categories (Gitsaki, 1996; Renouf & Sinclair, 1991), is another important criterion for MWU identification, which there is a lack of research. As discussed earlier, this would fall into the structural approach to understanding collocations. An example of colligation is counting the collocates 'early' and 'century' as 'early [year] century' when they occur with a variety of years between them, which would account for instances such as 'early twentieth century,' 'early nineteenth century,' etc., together. Table 2.6 below shows the advantage of processing corpus data with consideration for colligation. One thousand example sentences were collected from the COCA (Davies, 2008), and a concordance search identified the MWU most representative of how 'century' and 'earlier' occur together. One search was done with consideration for colligation, replacing every instance of a year with the marker [year]. By considering colligation, the top MWU identified was shown to have nearly double the frequency compared to the top MWU identified without consideration for colligation.

Table 2.6. A Comparison Between Two MWU Searches, One With and One Without Consideration for a Specific Type of Colligation

Without consideration for colligation		With consideration for colligation	
% of occurrences in 1,000 example sentences	MWU with co-occurrence of century and early	% of occurrences in 1,000 example sentences	MWU with co-occurrence of century and early
10.7%	century earlier	19.2%	early in the [year] century
9.5%	a century earlier	10.7%	century earlier
8.5%	early in this century	9.7%	early [year] century
7.3%	early in this century	9.5%	a century earlier
6.4%	centuries earlier	8.5%	early in this century
5.0%	early in the 20th century	8.3%	early as the [year] century
		8.3%	as early as the [year] century
		7.3%	early in the century
		6.4%	centuries earlier

However, depending on the research goal, colligation can potentially create more problems than it solves. For instance, when major content word categories, such as nouns or verbs, are replaced with colligational markers, the limitations of how a MWU can be formulated may not be conveyed to the learner. Take the colligational framework '[adjective] tea' for instance. Typical examples such as 'hot tea,' 'brown tea,' or 'strong tea' are perfectly logical, but explaining why 'powerful tea' is not an option becomes very difficult. Due to this idiosyncratic way collocations sometimes occur, grammar alone cannot determine which lexical items co-occur (Lewis, 2000a). Not specifying to the learner which adjectives are possible opens the door to errors occurring. This is why it is better to rely mainly on the lexical approach. However, colligation can still be a useful criterion to consider when attempting to identify high-frequency MWUs. Yet how this criterion can be implemented and the extent of its value remains to be seen. Therefore, my research aimed to clarify the value of specific types of colligational searches.

On the Value of Collocations

Nation (2001a) stated that a variety of knowledge is necessary to truly 'know' a word. This 'vocabulary depth' knowledge includes not only semantics, pronunciation, orthography, word parts, concepts, associations, grammar, and constraints on use but also a word's possible collocates. Several researchers believe that collocational knowledge is of significant value for the language learner. In fact, we have known about the value of collocational fluency for some time. Bolinger (1968) argued that we learn and memorize words in chunks. Later, he argued that most of our "manipulative grasp of words is by way of collocations" (Bolinger 1976, p. 8). Twaddell (1973) stated that teaching phrase-patterns and sentence patterns from the early stages of L2 learning may help vocabulary expansion. Among the other early advocates for the importance of collocations in L2 learning and their inclusion in L2 teaching is Brown (1974).

Collocational fluency has been referred to as a "decisive factor in developing fluency" (Almela & Sanchez, 2007, p. 37), and awareness of it is a matter of "first-rate importance" (McCarthy, 1984, p. 21). Durrant and Schmitt (2009) stated that "competent use of formulaic sequences is an important part of fluent and natural language use" (p. 157). Collocational fluency is not just important for advanced-level language processing, as Kjellmer (1987) stated that "collocations are indispensable and ubiquitous elements of any English text" (p. 133). Saville-Troike (1984) agreed, claiming they are essential even in the early stages of language learning.

In the past, fluency in formulaic language was considered of marginal importance (Ellis et al., 2008). However, many researchers have changed their view of its importance in recent years. Some researchers further assert that collocations are a central mechanism of how language organizes itself (Hoey, 2005). Lewis (1993) referred to this concept as 'grammaticalized lexis.' However, even if a stance is taken that collocations play a more insignificant role than that, many researchers still feel that mastery of its knowledge is essential for a learner to be considered fully fluent in a language (Bahns & Eldaw, 1993). Cowie (1992, p. 10) agreed, stating that "it is impossible to perform at a level acceptable to native users, in writing or speech, without controlling an appropriate range of MWUs." Ellis (1997) showed how the sentence 'I wish to be wedded to you' is syntactically possible but unnatural from a fluent speaker's perspective.

Previous research indicated that learning collocations is easier than learning words in isolation (Ellis, 2001; Lewis, 2000a; Taylor, 1983). For example,

Bogaards (2001) found that MWUs containing familiar words were retained 10% more than completely new single words immediately after a learning session and also 12.1% more in a delayed posttest three weeks later. But why are they easier? Laufer (1988) stated that collocations are useful in various levels of vocabulary acquisition and self-learning strategies. Schmitt (1997) explained how this is possible by presenting several different mnemonic strategies that learners can use. For example, one word in a MWU can serve as a mnemonic hook to help the learner remember the meaning of other words they have forgotten in the MWU.

Take the word 'spine,' for example. Imagine a situation where a second language learner learns the translation of the isolated word 'spine.' Then, imagine another student who learns the MWU 'injure my spine.' Now, imagine both students encountering the word in a reading passage without the word 'injure' and have forgotten its meaning. However, imagine that the student who studied the MWU remembers that spine occurs as 'injure my spine' despite still not remembering the meaning of 'spine.' If this student understands the meaning of 'injure,' they can deduce that 'spine' must mean some part of a person's body. Through this mnemonic hook, their brain can make the jump to remember the translation of 'spine,' while the student who studied the word in an isolated matter is left with no alternative but to give up. Furthermore, each time the student who learned the MWU makes that jump in their brain on their own, the connection between 'spine' and its translation becomes stronger and stronger, and eventually, they will not need to rely on 'injure' as a hook. In this way, the words of a MWU have the potential to aid learners in memory retrieval, thus strengthening connections and making learning more efficient overall.

In small-scale experiments, Chon and Shin (2009) and Boers et al. (2006) found the use of formulaic expressions correlated with perceived proficiency in fluent-speaker judgments of learners' L2 writing. Underwood et al. (2004) examined eye movements and found formulaic sequences to be read more quickly than non-formulaic equivalents. Conklin and Schmitt (2008) found similar results with self-paced reading tasks. Jiang and Nekrasova (2007) noted that grammatical judgments were faster and more accurate for formulaic language. Regarding production, both Dechert (1983) and Kuiper (1996) found the use of formulaic language made output smoother and more fluent. Hill (2000) agreed, stating that "collocation allows us to think more quickly and communicate more efficiently" (p. 54). Furthermore, when learners utilize prefabricated language, they free up processing time (Almela & Sanchez, 2007; Lewis, 1993; Nation, 2001a). Furukawa et al. (1998) found that teaching students to utilize a chunking learning strategy improved sixth-grade students' Stanford

Achievement test scores by an average of 6.15 points. Sinclair (1991) referred to this in his 'idiom principle' as making "fewer and larger choices" (p. 113).

On the Lack of Research and Resources

Collocations are also quite difficult to acquire because there is a lack of focus on directly teaching them. This stems from a lack of comprehensive resources. Nesselhauf (2005) wrote that "suggestions as to which individual collocations or groups of collocations that should be taught are scarce" (p. 254). One of the reasons why there is a lack of resources is there is a lack of comprehensive research. She also noted that much of the previous research does not go beyond simply stating that more emphasis on teaching collocations is needed. Hence, one reason why practitioners do not emphasize collocations despite being aware of their importance is that there are still very few studies that identify which are the most frequent (Durrant & Schmitt, 2009), and the studies that have been conducted all lack in comprehensiveness or are flawed in some way. For example, some available large-scale resources list items alphabetically instead of in frequency order. This prevents learners from studying more common items first. Issues such as this have resulted in the direct teaching of collocation being "marginalized in the language curriculum" (Wood, 2004, p. 28).

Another problem is the fact that much of previous research has limited its scope to a specific type of collocation or MWU. For instance, Biber et al. (2004) only found 172 'lexical bundles,' limiting themselves by a very conservative cut-off of 40 occurrences per million tokens and only considering four-word sequences. Simpson and Mendis' (2003) search for 'fixed, institutionalized, semantically opaque, academic idioms' only identified 238 such items. Aghbar (1990) and Bahns and Eldaw (1993) only examined verb-noun collocations, while Channell (1981) only looked at adjective-noun collocations. These studies produce results in stark contrast with claims that there are hundreds of thousands of collocations in a fluent speaker's lexicon.

While there is an abundance of collocation dictionaries available, they tend to present users with too much information. For instance, Kjellmer's (1994) collocation dictionary contains over 85,000 entries, and identifying the most useful collocations from such a large dataset is not an easy task. This lack of resources that specify useful collocations is thus clearly connected to the sheer number of items researchers must deal with. Shin's (2006) study was an excellent first step in alleviating these issues. Still, his study was limited since it only examined the most frequent 1,000 types in English. Hence, a more comprehensive list was still needed for general English when I began my research, and that was the gap in the literature that I aimed to fill.

Regarding larger resources, Ackermann and Chen's (2013) study identified approximately 2,400 MWUs. However, this resource has limitations in that the frequency data for each item was not released, and the items were listed alphabetically. So, for a learner who does not have time to study all of them and wants to study, for example, the first 500, they cannot study the most frequent (and therefore most useful) items first. Their study is also hampered by their not providing example sentences for learners to help them understand the contextual usage of the MWUs.

Both Eriksson (2012) and Byrd and Coxhead (2010) felt that contextual support is essential for understanding how to use MWUs. Eriksson (2012) stated that problems may occur if "activities highlight searches on a large number of bundles at the expense of appropriate levels of analysis" (p. 206). Woolard (2000) noted that teachers must become aware of the need to incorporate such co-textual information into their teaching. So, not only should learners be taught collocations directly in the form of MWUs, but they should also be given additional contextual support to help them master all the knowledge necessary to use MWUs properly. For instance, if 'pro bono' is taught, it would be ideal if a full contextual sentence accompanied it, bringing attention to the fact that the phrase is almost exclusively used as a legal term. Therefore, this is something that I considered in my research. For the approximately 11,000 general English I identified, my research team wrote original example sentences for each MWU to help learners acquire contextual knowledge of the items.

One study that did have several merits is Lei and Liu (2018). They started with a large number of pivot words (over 3,000), used the concgramming approach, and identified a significant number of MWUs (over 2,300). However, just like Morley (2015) and Ackermann and Chen (2013), their results were unfortunately presented alphabetically. Another issue was the fact that they only identified collocates that go with each pivot word in the following fashion: 'willingness, n; v + willingness; express, indicate.' Unfortunately, learners have to fill in the blanks, and it is unlikely that most would be able to do so accurately due to the aforementioned issue of the arbitrary nature of how words collocate.

A lack of collocation research and resources thus existed for general English, and my research focused on filling this gap. However, once the initial work began for my research, I began to see why such a lack of research and resources existed. Novel methodologies and software were required to accomplish the tasks necessary to improve upon existing resources. I also had to create large collaborative research teams of competent translators who worked for years to conduct L1-L2 congruency, among other barriers that needed to be traversed.

All of this proved extremely complex and challenging, and the steps I took to achieve these goals are detailed in Chapter 3 of this book.

On the Direct Teaching of Collocations

Researchers have recommended the direct study of collocations for some time now (Mackin, 1978; Marton, 1977). Likewise, Doughty and Williams (1998), Ellis (1994), and Koya (2004) all argued that collocations should be taught directly. In addition, Newman (1988) recommended the direct memorization of collocations, and Gitsaki (1996) recommended directly teaching them in class.

Although rote learning is often dismissed as outdated, the direct teaching of certain collocations may still be advantageous. Sokmen (1997) remarked that the anathema towards rote learning has actually led to decreased acquisition speed. Now, the pendulum is swinging back towards the middle for a more balanced approach. Shin (2006) agreed, stating that deliberate learning itself is not a problem but rather a "lack of balance with other ways of learning" (p. 163). In the past, discussion of more traditional methods such as paired associate learning has mainly focused on isolated vocabulary study. A vast majority of such research has shown such explicit study to be very efficient (Avery & Baker, 1997; Hopkins & Bean, 1999; Rodriguez & Sadoski, 2000). But what of collocations? Should we teach them directly as well? Chan and Liou (2005), Hsu (2002; 2005), Lien (2003), and Lin (2002; 2004) all found that such an approach towards teaching collocations was effective.

Foremost, teachers must expose students to useful collocations, thus enabling their acquisition. However, Nesselhauf's (2005) study revealed that exposure alone is insufficient. She argues that bringing attention to collocations is essential for developing fluency. If encounters are left to chance, then, as Wollard (2000) stated, "Learning will be extremely haphazard and inefficient" (p. 26). Lewis (2000b) remarked that it may be weeks, months, or even years before students re-encounter a particular collocation. Bahns and Sibilis (1992) found a similar issue in that mere exposure had little or no effect on improving collocational fluency in their study. Furthermore, approaches are often unsystematic when students are directly exposed to or taught collocations (Howarth, 1996).

Gairns and Redman (1986) remarked that teachers typically just deal with collocations as they appear in materials, which is inefficient and disorganized. They stated that this is not ideal, if effective at all. Biskup (1992) explained why this is, stating that "when encountering a new collocation, a learner does not make a conscious effort to understand or memorize it as it poses no specific perception problem to him or her" (p. 87). Lewis (2000b) and Wollard (2000) also agreed, stating that directly focusing on collocations will bring students' attention to high-frequency words that they are already familiar with but do not realize are occurring formulaically. Lewis (2000b) remarked that while he agrees "that learners should take responsibility for their own learning, they should not be taking responsibility for choosing which language items are more linguistically useful" (p. 18). Myers and Chang (2009) suggested that learners cannot simply gain collocational knowledge on their own and need some sort of guidance.

Some researchers have stated that L1-L2 incongruent collocations, in particular, should be taught directly (Bahns, 1993; Gairns & Redman, 1986). Laufer and Girsai (2008) found that students who studied using a contrastive analysis method outperformed meaning-focused and non-contrastive form-focused methods. They describe it as a "perfect 'pushed output' task that requires stretching one's linguistic resources" (p. 710) because it involves a higher involvement load.

Furthermore, since even advanced learners have been shown to have low collocational fluency, such students may need to learn how high-frequency vocabulary co-occurs despite having already mastered such isolated vocabulary's semantics. Lewis (2000b) echoed a similar remark, stating that "some students already know a lot of 'simple' words but are not aware of what those words can do for them because they haven't noticed their common collocations" (p. 24). In a related statement, Woolard (2000) wrote, "Learning more vocabulary is not just learning new words, it is often learning familiar words in new combinations" (p. 31).

From some perspectives, collocations themselves can be considered as 'words.' This is logical since evidence shows that they are stored in the brain in chunks in the same way that isolated vocabulary items are (Ellis, 1996; Wood, 2004; Wray, 2000). Hill (2000) agreed, stating that "in the same way that we teach individual words, we need to teach collocations. Rather than wait for students to meet common collocations for themselves, we need to present them in context just as we would present individual words" (p. 60). He thus suggests that every time a teacher teaches a new word, that word should be taught with its common collocate.

On Utilizing Corpus Data to Identify Collocations

Because of the sheer number of collocations and their learning burden mentioned above, researchers should attempt to use criteria to identify useful collocations with a high chance of error. However, in addition to the lack of a comprehensive list, many questions remain as to which criteria should be utilized to create one. In addition to semantic transparency discussed earlier, the following criteria can potentially isolate and identify specific collocations that are of value for learners.

There are various ways to identify useful collocations. The simplest and most common involves frequency data from a corpus (Biber et al., 1999; Hoey, 1991; Shin, 2006). While setting a frequency cut-off is "unavoidably arbitrary" (Nation, 2001a, p. 180), for teaching, a cut-off must be set regarding the practical limitation of how many items can be directly taught during limited classroom time. As mentioned earlier, many different frequency cut-offs have been used in collocation research, and there is still a lack of consensus on which is ideal. Biber et al. (2004) set their cut-off at 40 occurrences per million tokens, Cortez (2002) at 20, Biber et al. (1999) at ten, Kjellmer (1990) at four, Shin (2006) at three, and Kjellmer (1987) and Liu (2003) at two occurrences per million tokens. In Moon (1994), 70% of the MWUs examined occur less than once per million tokens. However, questions remain regarding how low a frequency cut-off can go and still contain mostly useful collocations.

Researchers have also utilized statistical measures of association, such as how Lorenz (1999) utilized MI data to identify high exclusive co-occurrence. However, MI can be problematic. MI emphasizes collocations whose components are not often found apart (Hunston, 2002; Stubbs, 1995). A good example would be 'crux' and 'matter.' In the COCA (Davies, 2008), data indicate that 'crux' and 'matter' have a very high MI of 7.24 (the corpus states that collocates with an MI of 3 or above should be considered semantically bonded). This is why when a fluent speaker is presented with the following cloze sentence, they can easily produce the answer:

> The crux of the m_____ is that our company needs to expand.

> However, despite having such a high MI, 'crux' and 'matter' have quite a low co-occurrence frequency. The pair only occurred 94 times in the 450 million tokens of the entire COCA.

> In comparison, the collocates 'call' and 'home' have a converse issue. Again, a fluent speaker would typically not have a problem completing the following cloze sentence:

> My parents always make me call h_____ if I'm going to be late.

When MI alone is used to identify collocates, such an example would be excluded. The collocation 'call' and 'home' has a very low MI score of only 0.42, with 1,218 occurrences in the corpus, over ten times as many occurrences as 'crux' and 'matter.' The reason 'call' and 'home' have such a low MI score, despite collocating, is that the words have high individual frequencies and frequently co-occur with a variety of other words. In fact, Shin (2006) found that MI was strongly related to frequency and has "no additional discriminating influence" (p. 59).

Kjellmer (1984) and Nation (2001a) stated that a collocation's dispersion, or its frequency of occurrence in various text categories, is necessary for identifying useful collocations. Other researchers added that when dealing with students studying particular topics or having specific goals, we should present collocations that occur only in a specific range (Conzett 2000; Woolard 2000). Such collocations can easily be identified when corpora provide dispersion data. Gries (2008) believes that dispersion data analysis is essential, stating that raw frequency data can be misleading regarding a word's general importance when the dispersion of its frequency data is unbalanced.

Dispersion has been a criterion utilized in the creation of word lists, such as Nation's (2004) BNC 3,000, and it has been referred to as an important criterion for vocabulary research (Nation & Webb, 2011). However, only a few small-scale studies on identifying useful collocations have utilized dispersion data from corpora to delimit their selections of useful collocations. One such study is Cortes (2002). However, its corpus consisted of only approximately 360,000 tokens. Biber et al. (2004) also employed dispersion criteria. However, their corpus consisted of only two million tokens. This is relatively small compared to the corpus used in my research (450 million tokens). Thus, research has not yet shown how dispersion data can be adequately applied to identify useful collocations with a large corpus.

Chronological stability over time may also be another important criterion for identifying useful collocations to study. Clearly, learners do not need to study collocations that are dated, which occurred only during a limited point in time, or that are not yet firmly established in the language. For example, the lemmas 'foreign' and 'Soviet' occurred in the COCA's (Davies, 2010) list of high-frequency collocates. However, the yearly breakdown of their occurrences in the COCA reveals that 88.4% of occurrences were from 1990-94. After that, occurrences fell to 5.6% in 1995-99, 2.7% in 2000-04, and 2.5% in 2005-2009. It is clear that these collocates were influenced by a particular political situation (the collapse of the Soviet Union) during a specific period. However, to date, no research has considered this criterion in regard to useful collocation identification. Therefore, the extent to which it can be applied as a useful criterion remains to be seen.

On Using L1-L2 Congruency to Identify Useful Collocations

Many researchers believe L1-L2 congruency to be an important criterion to consider when selecting useful collocations to directly focus on (Barghamadi et al., 2023; Du et al., 2021; Özdem-Ertürk, 2021). By studying incongruent MWUs, learners are given the necessary opportunities to focus on items with which they would otherwise have a high potential of making an error. Gyllstad (2005) gave the example of how, in German, the English 'take a photo' can be mistranslated as 'make a photo' because the German way to convey this (*ein Foto machen*) uses the verb *machen*, of which the English equivalent is 'make.' Zughoul (1991) gave another example of L1 interference from Arabic in that his students produced the following unnatural sentence: "the weather is kind in that country." Without such instruction, learners will typically directly translate from their L1 and thus produce unnatural-sounding formulations. In addition, identifying L1-L2 congruency can also improve the efficacy of learning. Bahns (1993) recommended not wasting time teaching L1-L2 congruent collocations. However, Biskup (1992) found that some learners will even be weary of congruent collocations. Nesselhauf (2003) agreed, stating that "congruent collocations cannot be ignored...mistakes are also made when collocations are congruent" (p. 238). Moon (1997) also agreed, giving the example of how even when MWUs are congruent in both the L1 and L2, "they are unlikely to be exact counterparts, and there may be different constraints on use" (p. 58).

Liu and Shaw's (2001) study gave a specific example of this. First, their study showed that learners produced significantly fewer collocations (1.6%) than fluent writers (12.1%). They postulated that the morphological differences between Chinese and English play a role in this. They gave the example of how there is a rule of inversion in English that leads to the formulation of 'film-making' from 'make a film' (inversion plus 'ing'). However, in Chinese, there is no inversion but the addition of the suffix *de*. So, *paidianying* becomes *paidianyingde*. Because of such differences between languages, they state that learners will avoid unfamiliar items or items without translation equivalents, which paves the way toward fossilization. Laufer and Eliasson (1993) echoed a similar opinion, reporting that L1-L2 incongruency was the best predictor of avoidance of using certain phrasal verbs.

Shin (2006) gave an example of how one L1 meaning can be represented by different forms in an L2. He also highlighted how one L2 form can have multiple meanings in the learner's L1. A commonly known example of this is how a significantly larger amount of words exist in languages in colder climates to describe various types of snow. In comparison, in warmer climates, all of these may be simply represented by one word.

In contrast, some researchers believe that the effect of a learner's L1 on attaining collocational fluency is marginal (Dechert & Lennon, 1989; Lennon, 1996; Ringbom, 1998). However, Nesselhauf (2003) found the opposite to be true. She stated that "the learners' L1 turns out to have a degree of influence that goes far beyond what earlier (small-scale) studies have predicted" (p. 223).

However, there is still a lack of research regarding the extent to which L1-L2 congruency is an issue in learning collocations. For example, due to time constraints, Shin (2006) could only examine approximately 10% of the English collocations in his study for congruency with Korean. However, his study still found that L1-L2 congruency was an important factor to consider in that one-third of the items examined were incongruent. Regardless, Gitsaki (1996) stated that "syntagmatic relations are more likely to differ from language to language" (p. 3). She gave the example of how the Greek learners in her study had specific problems with collocations that contained a preposition since the Greek language has many that do not coincide with English. Therefore, researchers should conduct a contrastive analysis of the learners' L1 in question. Nesselhauf (2005) said that conducting such studies is "desirable" (p. 272). Liu and Shaw (2001) also recommended such studies to produce "customized syllabi applicable to teaching L2 learners of specific mother tongues" (p. 189). Therefore, my research took on this challenge regarding the examination of Japanese, Chinese, and Korean congruency with English collocations.

Conclusion

In conclusion, this chapter has shown that there is still considerable disagreement and gaps in the research concerning collocations. It was shown that there are various ways to define and approach collocations, with each having strong and weak points depending on the research goal. Out of the previous approaches taken toward understanding and defining collocations, the lexical approach and some aspects of the structural approach were ideal for my research goals. The approach of using frequency of co-occurrence as the main criterion for identifying collocations was found to be ideal for achieving these goals, and it was also shown that identifying collocations by counting words as lemmas was preferable to types or word families.

This literature review has also shown that if a study is to be second language learner-focused, then rigid classification and definition of collocations as distinct and separate from free combinations is not ideal because of factors such as L1-L2 congruency, among others. In regard to word counting and MWU identification, concgramming was shown to be the best approach to count co-occurrence most reliably for my research's goal. Using fluent speaker intuition was also found to be the best option to identify MWUs most representative of lemmatized concgrams to provide learners with the most useful information on how collocates are typically used without overloading them with too much information. The value of consideration for colligation was also highlighted.

In general, previous research views collocational knowledge as a priority and of significant importance for obtaining fluency in a second language. They are a major part of any language and occur ubiquitously in any text, and some researchers believe that the vast majority of the language we speak occurs in chunks. Some researchers actually view collocation as the central organizer of language itself.

Previous research indicated that collocations are of high value to learners and thus worth focusing on. Researchers have found that collocational fluency helps learners read quicker and make grammatical judgments quicker and more accurately. They also found that output was smoother and more fluent. So, compared to learning isolated vocabulary and decoding or encoding information word by word, being aware of collocational relationships between words should enable learners to process language more efficiently. Furthermore, the concept of mnemonic hooks highlighted how learning MWUs can be easier than learning isolated vocabulary items. It is, therefore, logical to study vocabulary via MWUs instead of isolated vocabulary since they have a lower learning burden.

However, researchers revealed a severe lack of collocational fluency among second language learners from various backgrounds. Learners from Asia, the Middle East, and Europe were all shown to lack collocational fluency, even those with advanced fluency. In fact, collocational knowledge was shown not to improve as learners improved upon other aspects of fluency. Many researchers indicated that the vast majority of errors learners made were collocational. Multiple researchers also found that approximately 50 % of the collocations learners produce were either deviant or wrong.

If many learners lack collocational fluency, then it is only logical to investigate why this is. Many researchers point out various issues that lead to a high learning burden for collocations. First, the substantial quantity of collocations a learner must master is a significant barrier since some researchers believe that hundreds of thousands of collocations exist. Other researchers point out that the way collocations are formulated is also very complex and often arbitrary. It is also very easy for learners to make errors by over-generalizing or underusing certain collocations.

Another aspect of collocations that makes them difficult to learn was shown to be semantic transparency. Some researchers found that semantically restricted collocations were more challenging to learn, while others indicated that learners also struggle with literal collocations. Several researchers identified types of collocations that learners from specific backgrounds struggled with. For instance, Taiwanese students struggled with verb-noun collocations especially, and when they did, most of the errors were with the verb.

The next step to examining why learners lack collocational fluency I took was to examine whether or not there is a lack of research and resources and a lack of focus in second language instruction. In fact, previous research indicated that these gaps in the research exist. Collocations were found not to be taught directly to students, although several researchers believed that this would be ideal. Teachers have also been aware of the value of collocations and that they should be taught directly for some time now, but despite this, they still are not. This is because there is still a lack of quality, large-scale research and resources to use as a reference for such instruction.

Previous research has also limited the scope of what was examined so severely that no comprehensive, reliable resource exists for direct instruction. This stems from the large amounts of data that need to be analyzed to produce such a resource and a lack of consensus on how such an analysis should be conducted.

Previous research also indicated a lack of consensus regarding the criteria that should be used in such an analysis. However, many researchers agree that frequency of co-occurrence is an important criterion to consider. Because of the hundreds of thousands of collocations that exist, setting a frequency cut-off, while unavoidably arbitrary, is necessary. Which cut-off is best is a question that remains unanswered, though.

In addition, the semantic transparency of collocations is another important criterion to consider. However, it remains to be seen what percentage of high-frequency collocations are semantically transparent or not. Moreover, the issue of L1-L2 congruency can make the criterion of semantic transparency moot. Another criterion mentioned above that can also be problematic is MI. Previous researchers have not only found it to be unreliable, but they also found it to have no discriminating influence in comparison to frequency. Using dispersion data is another criterion that many researchers agree is important. Such data helped identify collocations that occur across a wide variety of languages, thus helping to identify only truly useful items.

Furthermore, using dispersion data in addition to frequency data helps avoid being misled by raw frequencies of items that only occur in one type of language, such as academic language. Chronological data was also shown to be an important criterion to consider, but this literature review has shown that research is lacking concerning its usefulness as a criterion. Another essential criterion mentioned was L1-L2 congruency. A wide variety of researchers agreed that this is an important criterion to consider when the aim is to identify collocations with a higher learning burden for learners and thus need additional focus. Thus, my previous research aimed to address all of these gaps in the research.

In conclusion, a wide variety of researchers agree that collocations are valuable and should be taught directly, but that they aren't, and learners thus lack collocational fluency. There is a lack of research and resources in several areas, and many questions remain about how to conduct and create such research. This book will hereafter explain how my research filled these major gaps to achieve the ultimate goal of creating resources that teachers and learners can use for the direct study of collocations.

Chapter 3

Addressing Gaps in the Research

Introduction

Previous research indicates a lack of a large-scale resource identifying high-frequency collocations worthy of direct instruction or study. Examining why this gap in the research exists and how it could be solved makes it clear why it has yet to be filled.

First, a reliable methodology had yet to be identified, and thus, a significant amount of time during my Ph.D. thesis (Rogers, 2017a) was spent creating and testing such a methodology. Some methods used proved fruitful, while others did not. Since some were highly complex and time-consuming, the results should be helpful for future researchers to avoid spending time taking steps that are not worthwhile. Furthermore, as each step was taken towards identifying and testing the collocations, some discoveries were made, requiring the rethinking and planning of my project's approach. For instance, to accomplish one particular task, the software necessary did not even exist, and an expert in the field had to be relied upon to create custom software specifically for this part of my research.

Second, the sheer amount of data needed to be analyzed was staggering. No one researcher could accomplish such a task. This necessitated the creation of research teams consisting of volunteer data collectors, analyzers, and translators. For instance, any collocation worthy of direct study should have balanced dispersion, but such data was not readily available in an easy-to-analyze form from the corpus used. Therefore, such data had to be manually copied and pasted from an online corpus for over 10,000 collocations. Another example of why such a team of volunteers was necessary was how not all collocations have an equal learning burden. For instance, when collocations are said differently in a learner's mother tongue, such items will have a much higher learning burden (L1-L2 incongruency). So, if a specific group of learners is to be tested on their knowledge of the collocations identified, a balanced selection of items needs to be taken with such issues as L1-L2 congruency in mind. The only way to achieve this is for each collocation to be translated into the L1 in question, compared, and rated regarding its congruency. This created the necessity to translate and compare over 10,000 items, a task that could only be done by several volunteers, which took a significant amount of time since the goal was to create resources for Japanese, Chinese, and Korean learners.

With these above issues in mind, it became evident that my research goals were ambitious, and practical limitations prevented them from being accomplished in the past. However, as stated above, considerable effort and several novel solutions were taken to overcome these obstacles. Thus, the results were quite interesting and should be considered a valuable contribution to the literature.

The Gaps in the Research

The following research questions constitute gaps in the research that I have answered in my Ph.D. thesis or subsequent research I have conducted:

1. What is an ideal corpus frequency data cut-off for identifying MWUs?

2. Is corpus dispersion data analysis useful for identifying MWUs?

3. Is corpus chronological data analysis useful for identifying MWUs?

4. Is consideration for colligation an important criterion for identifying MWUs?

5. What percentage of MWUs is deemed by fluent speakers worthy of expanding beyond their most frequent exemplar?

6. What percentage of MWUs most representative of high-frequency lemmatized concgrams has low semantic transparency?

7. What percentage of MWUs most representative of high-frequency lemmatized concgrams has low L1-L2 congruency with Japanese, Chinese, and Korean?

8. Is fluent speaker intuition reliable regarding high-frequency vocabulary usage in context creation?

9. What is Japanese university students' knowledge of MWUs most representative of high-frequency lemmatized concgrams?

Research Methods and Techniques

Research Paradigm

The overarching approach to my research was post-positivist in that the nature of the research must employ measures that approximate reality while admittedly possessing unavoidable weaknesses. For instance, it is impossible to choose a high-frequency count cut-off and unequivocally show that any occurrence below that particular number is a low-frequency item. Nation (2001a) states that setting such a frequency cut-off is unavoidably arbitrary but necessary to delimit what should be taught directly. Furthermore, a post-positivist approach also assumes that one singular answer is attainable and is not preoccupied with multiple perspectives. It also avoids the pitfalls of breaking down collocations into more and more restricted categories and instead aims to find one answer: What are the most frequent collocations worthy of direct study? Such an approach, which employs quantitative analysis to discover the best approximation of reality, is ideal for such a study. The method frees itself from the inadequacies of black-and-white thinking by admitting that results will never be unequivocal but rather be the best approximation possible within unavoidable constraints.

The first step in my research was an examination of a corpus to identify high-frequency MWUs. It aimed first to identify the necessary criteria for inclusion and use these criteria to find the most useful collocational lemma pairs. It also aimed to devise a methodology to find the most frequent MWU these lemma pairs occur in to help present them to language learners in the most useful contexts. Using lemmas instead of word types, as Shin (2006) did, is unique compared to some previous research and an improvement because of its ability to consolidate data. So, MWUs such as 'take a walk,' 'took a walk,' and 'taking walks' can be counted as one 'item.' Listing them separately (using types) and presenting them to students at separate times (due to frequency differences) would make an already copious amount of data even more excessive and make for less efficient learning since learning the exemplary unit of such items is ideal. Semantic transparency and contrastive analysis were also conducted to help identify items students need to spend the most time on and to reduce the overall learning load. Finally, testing Japanese university students' knowledge of a balanced sample of these items helped confirm the approach's validity.

Just as many language models are complementary, rather than any singular model being a definitive paradigm, my research drew from more than one approach to examine all pertinent aspects regarding collocation. It drew from the structural approach only when it was appropriate to deal with MWUs whose counts are strongly affected by colligation while mainly being driven by the lexical approach's tenet of the importance of raising students' awareness of lexis and how words combine to help them attain fluency.

Data Source, Collection Methodology, and Analysis

One of the most useful resources for identifying common collocations/MWUs is corpora (Meijs, 1992; Noel, 1992; Francis, 1993). But which corpus should be used for the identification of high-frequency collocations? Shin (2006) stated that a large corpus with a large variety of texts is essential for producing reliable data. Thus, Kjellmer's (1994) use of the 1-million-token Brown Corpus (Nelson and Kucera, 1979) may not have produced the most reliable data despite it being one of the largest, most reliable corpora at the time. Through computer technology, more extensive corpora have been compiled. In recent years, many researchers have relied on the 100- million-token British National Corpus (1994), or BNC, for collocational research (e.g., Durrant & Schmitt, 2009; Shin, 2006). However, the BNC stopped being developed in 1993 and has been referred to as past its sell-by date (Kilgarriff et al., 2007). Davies' (2008) COCA can be considered a better choice as it is four times larger than the BNC and is still being added to today. Furthermore, it has a wide and balanced dispersion regarding genres and spoken versus written content. In addition, it consists of American English, which is the variety of English that my research team members speak. This is also the variety of English mainly taught to Japanese learners, the L1 group that my research initially intended to create a resource for.

My research examined lemma collocates of Davies' (2010) most frequent 5,000 lemma list derived from the entire COCA (Davies, 2008). This list consists of nearly 800,000 collocations. It was then delimited by a frequency cut-off of approximately one occurrence per million tokens (500 occurrences in the corpus), and only content words (nouns, verbs, adjectives, and adverbs) were included in the analysis. The list was then delimited to include items with an MI score of three or more. These three criteria resulted in a list consisting of 25,969 lemma pairs. Next, the COCA corpus was utilized to collect example sentences for these pairs to aid in identifying MWUs most representative of the lemma pairs. The corpus was also used to collect chronological and genre dispersion data to aid in identifying only items with balanced data dispersion.

The COCA's (2008) online interface was utilized to search for chronological and genre dispersion data and example sentences for each collocational lemma pair. Anthony's (2013) AntWordPairs, custom software written specifically for this part of my research, was then used to examine 500 example sentences in which each pair occurred to extract the most frequent MWU most exemplary of those lemmas. This method revealed the most common MWU two lemmas occur, such as how 'take a walk' is the exemplar of the lemma 'take' and 'walk,' as discussed above. From two to seven-word MWUs were searched for, and only MWUs that occur in more than 5% of the total were included.

All items were also examined for colligational issues. Data were first examined to determine what kind of colligational issues exist, such as how it may be beneficial to replace items such as days of the week, ordinal and cardinal numbers, etc., with a unifying marker to allow their occurrences to be counted together. Then, GoTagger (Goto, 2005) and Textcrawler (2011) were used together to adjust such items. Homonyms were adjusted as well using these two pieces of software.

Duplicate entries were then manually removed from items delimited by part of speech and frequency in Davies' (2010) list. Duplicates occur when a collocate also happens to be a high-frequency lemma. For example, 'take' may exist in the list of pivot words used to search for collocates, and one of the collocates identified may be 'break.' However, 'break' may also exist somewhere in the pivot word list as well, thus creating duplicate entries of the collocations 'take/break' and 'break/take.'

Then, chronological and dispersion data for the remaining pairs using the COCA's (Davies, 2008) online interface was collected, and only items deemed to have balanced dispersion of data were kept. Next, for each pair from the COCA, 500 example sentences were collected, which were then used for collocational exemplar searches using AntWordPairs (Anthony, 2013).

Subsequently, data regarding Japanese first-year university students' knowledge of the general English collocational exemplars was collected. An attempt was made to test as many students as possible (approximately 500) from the same university. An attempt was also made to test students from as wide of a range of proficiencies as possible, and their proficiencies were confirmed by the collection of their TOEFL score data. Since it is well-known that Japanese students have far superior visual recognition vs. aural recognition skills in English, the proposed test was a visual diagnostic test to determine the highest possible familiarity with the items. Productive skill was measured by taking a direct approach, and thus, students were tested with productive cloze questions. Test questions were balanced regarding item frequency and L1-L2 congruency to help determine whether these factors play a role in determining student knowledge. This test was also discrete point, making every effort only to test collocational fluency and not any other language skills. Specifically, no supporting context words in the cloze sentences went beyond the most frequent 3,000 word families of English. Furthermore, only the least frequent collocate in the collocation was the target item to answer. In addition, the first letter of the target item was provided to avoid other answers. When this did not suffice, and there were still other possible answers, more letters were provided. The need for this was determined by validating the test with fluent speakers to ensure that the example sentences were sufficient for prompting the correct collocate.

The MWUs identified were also rated for semantic transparency. Grant and Bauer's (2004) taxonomy, which broke down MWUs into literals, figuratives, ONCEs, and core idioms, was utilized to judge semantic transparency. Items not falling into the above categories were also marked as such.

Then, an example sentence was written for each MWU, and both the MWU and the sentence were translated into Japanese, Chinese, and Korean. Next, contrastive analysis was conducted to rate the L1-L2 congruency of the MWUs and translations in these languages.

Next, frequency data were examined to ensure that the resulting MWUs and their example sentences did not constitute a learning burden that is not practical.

Finally, the test data was analyzed to determine whether or not student proficiency level, MWU frequency, or L1-L2 congruency played a role in determining student knowledge. Note that semantic transparency was not a criterion considered since the vast majority of the MWUs examined were deemed literals. Thus, a balanced selection of items (literals, ONCEs, figuratives, and core idioms) was impossible.

Filling the Gaps in the Research

What is an Ideal Corpus Frequency Data Cut-off for Identifying High-frequency General English MWUs?

Because of the large number of MWUs, determining a frequency cut-off is necessary to identify the most useful MWUs of general English to teach or study directly. Biber et al. (2004) set a self-admittedly conservative cut-off at 40 occurrences per million. Cortez (2002) limited examined items to 20 occurrences per million tokens, Biber et al. (1999) considered up to ten occurrences, Shin (2006) examined as low as three occurrences, and Kjellmer (1987) collected data for items occurring two times per million. However, questions remain as to how low a frequency cut-off can go and still contain mostly useful collocations. Thus, the following experiment determined an ideal corpus frequency data cut-off for identifying MWUs most representative of high-frequency lemmatized concgrams.

In this experiment, the source for collocational lemma pairs was Davies' (2010) Word List Plus Collocates, which consists of 739,254 lemma congrams. It was compiled using frequency data from the 450 million token COCA tagged with the CLAWS 7 part of speech tag set (University Centre for Computer

Corpus Research on Language, n.d.) and only included collocates with three or more occurrences. It consists of the most frequent lemma pairs that co-occur with the most frequent 5,000 lemmas in the corpus. Cobb's (2013) program Vocabprofile was used for data analysis.

Davies' (2010) collocation list was utilized as a starting point, and a frequency cut-off was set. Nation (2001a) suggested 2,000 word families as "practical and feasible" (p. 96) in regard to direct teaching, while Nation (2001b) suggested a limit of 3,000 word families. Therefore, assuming the collocations selected were deemed useful, I aimed for 2-3,000 word families.

Various frequency cut-offs were piloted to determine how many useful collocations each level had. The study began at the highest cut-off set by Biber et al. (2004) of 40 occurrences per million tokens and progressed to Kjellmer's (1987) two occurrences per million. Then, the 25,000-word family BNC and COCA list in Vocabprofile (Cobb, 2013) was utilized to determine how many word families the collocations consisted of to ensure that those selected did not exceed 3,000 word families.

Only content words (nouns, verbs, adjectives, adverbs) were considered. Duplicate entries were also removed since the collocation was often a pivot word within Davies' (2010) most frequent 5,000 lemmas. A fluent speaker then judged the 'usefulness' of a sample of the pairs to ensure that the list was not overly inclusive.

The cut-off of two occurrences per million tokens utilized in Davies (2010) resulted in a list of lemma pairs consisting of only 1,874 families plus off-list types. Thus, a more inclusive cut-off was considered, given the pedagogically feasible goal of teaching between 2,000 and 3,000 word families (Nation, 2001a; 2001b). Pairs occurring once per million tokens comprised 2,789 families plus off-list types, and pairs occurring once per 500,000 tokens comprised 4,778 families[1]. Therefore, the cut-off of one occurrence per million tokens was tentatively determined to be ideal.

When the lemma pairs remaining at this cut-off point were processed with Vocabprofile (Cobb, 2013), it was found that these covered 83.14% of the top 3,000 word families (see Table 3.1 below). Also of note is the fact that 96.74% of the tokens in the lemma pair list occur within the top 3,000 word families.

---

[1] The data set was too large to be processed via Vocabprofile and thus Heatley et al.'s (2002) RANGE program was utilized instead for this file. It should be noted that both programs function identically and use the same BNC/COCA combined reference data.

Table 3.1. Word Frequency Breakdown of Lemma Pairs Occurring Once Per Million Tokens According to Vocabprofile's 25,000-word Families of the BNC and COCA

Freq. Level	Families (%)	Types (%)	Tokens (%)	Cumulative token %
K-1 Words	887 (32.46)	1,247 (36.00)	17,277 (68.38)	68.38
K-2 Words	757 (27.70)	968 (27.94)	4,924 (19.49)	87.87
K-3 Words	628 (22.98)	721 (20.81)	2,242 (8.87)	**96.74**
K1-K3 Coverage				**83.14**
K-4 Words	240 (8.78)	247 (7.13)	399 (1.58)	98.32
K-5 Words	114 (4.17)	114 (3.29)	154 (0.61)	98.93
K-6 Words	51 (1.87)	54 (1.56)	71 (0.28)	99.21
K-7 Words	19 (0.70)	19 (0.55)	22 (0.09)	99.30
K-8 Words	16 (0.59)	16 (0.46)	18 (0.07)	99.37
K-9 Words	8 (0.29)	8 (0.23)	9 (0.04)	99.41
K-10 Words	2 (0.07)	2 (0.06)	2 (0.01)	99.42
K-11 Words	5 (0.18)	5 (0.14)	9 (0.04)	99.46
K-12 Words	1 (0.04)	1 (0.03)	1 (0.00)	99.46
K-13 Words	1 (0.04)	1 (0.03)	1 (0.00)	99.46
K-14 Words	2 (0.07)	2 (0.06)	2 (0.01)	99.47
K-15 Words				
K-16 Words				
K-17 Words	2 (0.07)	2 (0.06)	2 (0.01)	99.48
K-18 Words				
K-19 Words				
K-20 Words				
K-21 Words				
K-22 Words				
K-23 Words				
K-24 Words				
K-25 Words				
Off-List:				100.00
Total				100.00
Total word families found (2,733) plus off-list types (56)				**2,789**

Note. 'K' represents 1,000 word families. So, K-1 equals 1-1,000 most frequent word families, K-2 1,001-2,000, and so on.

This one occurrence per million cut-off resulted in a list of 25,969 lemma pairs. However, many duplicate entries existed in this list because sometimes the collocate of a pivot word also happened to be a pivot word itself. For instance, the lemma pairs 'indicate/clearly' and 'clearly/indicate' both exist in the list. Such instances were manually checked for, and many of them were found and removed. In addition, any proper nouns, noise in the data, and language unsuitable or useful for the target learner group (such as inappropriate language like profanity or language related to sex) were also scanned for manually and removed.

Chronological data dispersion and range dispersion issues were not considered at this stage because these two criteria were planned to be examined later. This resulted in a list of 12,615 pairs being identified. Due to the large number of items, this list was scanned for general usefulness by an experienced teacher of English, and the vast majority were found useful and worthy of direct teaching. Therefore, it was confirmed that the frequency cut-off was ideal.

The frequency cut-off utilized resulted in excellent coverage of high-frequency vocabulary, in that 96.75% of the lemma pairs identified fell within the top 3,000 word families. The lemma pairs also exhibited good coverage of the top 3,000 word families, with 83.14% of the word families represented in the lemma pair list.

However, the large number of items identified presents a challenge. The vast majority of items were deemed useful, even in the lower frequency range of one occurrence per million running words. In fact, I found that useful collocations can still be found as low as one occurrence per hundred thousand tokens, such as 'nice/vacation,' 'finish/workout,' and 'tend/exaggerate' (Davies, 2010). However, setting a more inclusive frequency cut-off would create a list of more than 2-3,000 word families, which would not be practical in direct instruction. This abundance of useful items poses a serious barrier to both research and the study of collocation/MWUs. Therefore, further steps must be taken to focus on items with a higher learning burden or items that are more useful for specific learning contexts. Such steps include dispersion data, L1 congruency, and semantic transparency analyses.

Determining the extent to which frequency data can help inform useful collocation selection revealed both potential and limitations. First, it was shown that it is possible to set a frequency cut-off that results in a list of collocations that can be practically taught. What at first seemed an impractical number of items to teach was, in reality, only 2,789 word families combined in 12,615 different ways, which is within the 2,000 to 3,000 word family estimate of what is considered possible to be taught directly. While many useful collocations do occur beyond the frequency cut-off utilized, the resulting list of collocations showed excellent coverage of high-frequency vocabulary (83.14%) in addition to having 96.74% of the word families within the pairs being within the most frequent 3,000 word families.

Although the results were promising, a number of issues still needed to be addressed. Removing duplicates (instances when a collocate of one pivot word is also a pivot word) had to be conducted. This is an essential step, but it must be done manually, and thus it is time-consuming. Moreover, proper nouns also need to be removed. This step is also time-consuming because it must be done manually. Judging whether a lemmatized collocational pair is part of a larger proper noun was also difficult without examining concordance data. So, this experiment was just one step in a larger process toward creating a resource to help learners attain collocational fluency.

Is Corpus Dispersion Data Reliable for Identifying High-frequency General English MWUs?

Because of the large number of collocations, researchers such as Nation (2001) recommended delimiting items selected for direct study to those with the highest value for learners. If a learner's goal is to master general English, then that learner should only focus on collocations that occur in a balanced way among various genres. Researchers recommend using this as a criterion for direct study item selection. However, it remains to be seen how corpus data can specifically be used to accomplish this task. So, the following experiment determined whether or not corpus dispersion data is reliable for identifying MWUs most representative of high-frequency lemmatized concgrams.

In this experiment, the data source was the 12,615 lemmatized concgrams identified in the previous experiment. Dispersion data for each concgram was sourced from the COCA (Davies, 2008). Its interface allows users to extract dispersion data for five genres: spoken, fiction, magazine, newspaper, and academic. The interface also allows for the extraction of chronological data in four-year increments: 1990-94, 1995-99, 2000-04, 2005-09, and 2010-12. Since the four-year section 2010-13 was yet to be completed during this experiment, its data were not included.

A range of parameters for determining balanced distribution within the corpus used was tested due to the gap in research. As with frequency cut-offs, any cut-off set for dispersion or chronological data will be unavoidably arbitrary. For instance, Hwang and Nation (1995) specifically stated that their choice of vocabulary occurring in 10 out of 15 sections of the corpora in their study for balanced dispersion was unavoidably arbitrary. Ackermann and Chen (2013) also arbitrarily used the inclusion criteria for identifying collocations of their being in five or more texts in their dataset. Deciding on a parameter that unequivocally designates a collocation as having a balanced or unbalanced

Addressing Gaps in the Research

dispersion distribution is clearly impossible. Therefore, experiments were conducted with parameters that best approximated balanced distribution.

The parameters I utilized required that a specific percentage of the total occurrences had to occur in a majority of the COCA's genres: three or more out of the five genres. Fluent speaker intuition was used to determine the best percentage cut-off. The lemma list was examined for items that seemed specialized, and some of these items were found to have approximately 5% or less of their occurrences in three or more of the genres. Hence, dispersion data were analyzed at three separate percentages to determine the most useful parameter: less than 10%, 5%, and 2.5% of total occurrences in three or more genres. Then, pairs flagged at these parameters were examined to determine if they seemed specialized by a fluent speaker and, therefore, would not be worthy of direct instruction for a learner studying general English.

To accomplish this, all flagged items in the list were analyzed to determine if the parameters could not identify specialized items. Ideally, multiple examiners should have been used, but this was not possible at the time due to time constraints. Therefore, I conducted the initial analysis myself. To determine the extent to which the dispersion data distribution cut-offs identified items not worthy of direct instruction, the collocates were judged regarding their usefulness. Each item was given a rating (see Table 3.2 below) in regard to its value for learners of general English.

Table 3.2. Criteria for Rating the Value of Collocates for Learners of General English

Rating	Value in Regard to Direct Teaching for Learners of General English
1	Provides no value whatsoever if directly taught
2	Provides little value if directly taught
3	Provides questionable value if directly taught
4	Provides value but with limitations if directly taught
5	Provides clear value if directly taught

After being rated, any items flagged by each cut-off parameter rated 1 or 2 were tallied. Furthermore, any items not flagged by the cut-off parameters that received ratings of 1 or 2 were also tallied. These two steps were then used to judge the cut-off parameter's ability to identify collocations that are of little or no use for general learners of English regarding balanced dispersion and chronological data. Finally, all items identified as being unbalanced that were not flagged were examined to determine if they fell into a common genre (e.g., academic language).

Out of all three parameters tested, the 2.5% or more cut-off in three or more genres was the most reliable regarding the appropriate flagging of items of little use for learners of general English (Figure 3.1 below). The 2.5 parameter was also the lowest regarding total items either erroneously flagged or judged unbalanced by a fluent speaker, which were not flagged (Figure 3.2 below). The most reliable parameter was at 2.5%, where 347 of the 720 items flagged (48.1%) were judged to be accurately flagged by fluent speakers. The next most reliable parameter was at 5%, where a total of 538 of the 1,426 items flagged (37.7%) were judged to be accurately flagged by fluent speakers. The most unreliable parameter was at 10%, where a total of 664 of the 3,193 items flagged (20.8%) were judged to be accurately flagged by fluent speakers.

Figure 3.1. Percentage of Items Accurately and Erroneously Flagged for Balanced Dispersion Data Distribution at All Three Parameters

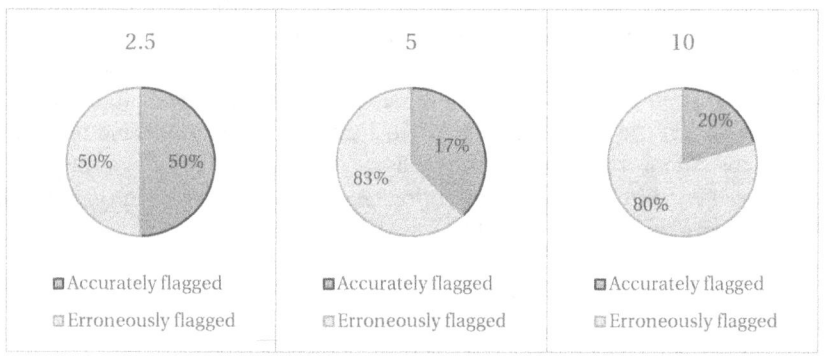

Figure 3.2. Total Items Erroneously Flagged or Judged Unbalanced Which Were Not Flagged

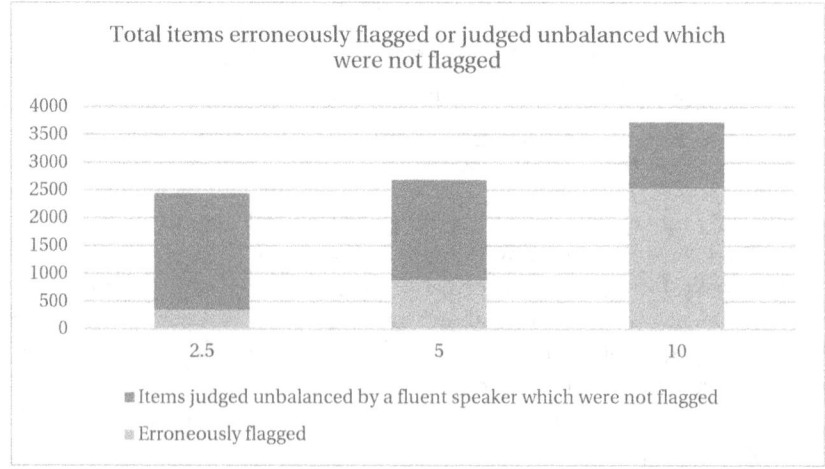

At the 2.5% parameter, 2,088 items were not flagged, which were considered to have low value for learners of general English for lack of balanced dispersion. At the 5% parameter, 1,788 items were not flagged, and at the 10% parameter, 1,193 items were not flagged. In addition to the above results, other discoveries were made when fluent speakers analyzed the entire list of items. Certain items were deemed to be not worthy of inclusion for learners of general English because they were either inappropriate language (language related to sex, profanity, etc.), grammatical formulations ('so/and'), duplicates (how 'disease/transmitted' and 'disease/sexually' both result in the most common MWU identified being 'sexually transmitted disease'), and compound nouns ('log cabin,' 'peanut butter,' etc.). The totals can be seen in Table 3.3 below.

Table 3.3. Items Found Not to be Worthy of Inclusion Because They Were Either Inappropriate Language, Grammatical Formulations, Duplicates, or Compound Nouns

Inappropriate	Grammatical	Duplicates	Compound Nouns
15	200	407	129

When a fluent speaker judged items to determine their type of specialized language, four specific types accounted for the vast majority of items: scientific language, descriptive language primarily used in fiction, language related to food, and language used primarily on television. Table 3.4 below gives five samples of the items flagged in each of the four most common types of language at all three parameters.

Table 3.4. Samples of Items Flagged for Having Unbalanced Dispersion in Each of the Four Most Common Genres at All Three Parameters

Pair	Parameter	Type	Spo.	Fic.	Mag.	News.	Acad.
control/locus	2.5	scientific	0	1	7	1	888
standard/deviation	2.5	scientific	2	4	42	26	2,412
variable/dependent	2.5	scientific	0	0	3	0	2,160
analysis/regression	2.5	scientific	6	1	14	5	1,707
study/longitudinal	2.5	scientific	7	2	64	7	901
slice/thinly	2.5	food	5	5	1,208	402	0
large/skillet	2.5	food	1	6	1,080	347	2
carbohydrate/gram	2.5	food	12	0	567	805	6

flour/cup	2.5	food	0	11	882	484	0
heat/simmer	2.5	food	2	3	833	414	5
lip/lick	2.5	descriptive	13	584	53	9	9
head/jerk	2.5	descriptive	4	597	36	10	4
face/turn	2.5	descriptive	40	1,583	105	44	44
hand/slide	2.5	descriptive	9	644	79	12	11
arm/touch	2.5	descriptive	14	623	52	13	11
moment/commercial	2.5	television	2,785	4	0	0	1
begin/clip	2.5	television	5,874	4	3	8	1
break/welcome	2.5	television	1,250	1	5	6	0
join/studio	2.5	television	829	2	9	16	1
continue/prime-time	2.5	television	510	0	2	1	1
status/socioeconomic	5	scientific	20	8	46	34	998
population/density	5	scientific	16	5	95	29	499
representative/sample	5	scientific	20	5	58	10	499
social/structure	5	scientific	47	38	174	60	1,169
model/predict	5	scientific	30	6	125	33	485
cup/sugar	5	food	40	69	2,836	1,317	2
fat/saturated	5	food	107	9	1,656	2,409	33
heat/medium	5	food	9	4	2,694	983	3
cup/butter	5	food	11	23	1,442	465	0
teaspoon/vanilla	5	food	10	12	1,096	442	0
head/cock	5	descriptive	10	1,057	81	28	7
lip/purse	5	descriptive	5	715	49	15	5
head/tilt	5	descriptive	19	1,311	169	46	26
lip/bite	5	descriptive	29	1,065	53	38	10
mouth/corner	5	descriptive	10	856	72	20	21
commercial/break	5	television	17,903	50	55	45	5
morning/join	5	television	1,770	22	25	30	6
report/correspondent	5	television	712	0	24	47	10
today/guest	5	television	548	17	17	13	0
continue/commercial	5	television	639	4	20	25	23
social/science	10	scientific	80	37	294	277	3,310

Addressing Gaps in the Research

waste/solid	10	scientific	26	9	232	138	1,426
social/order	10	scientific	19	56	184	71	1,022
management/water	10	scientific	9	2	59	59	585
soil/erosion	10	scientific	9	3	124	32	396
juice/lemon	10	food	151	80	2,640	1,352	12
high/heat	10	food	64	45	1,461	555	51
oil/large	10	food	117	30	1,141	526	148
acid/fatty	10	food	36	2	912	76	196
large/pot	10	food	7	81	611	358	33
eye/roll	10	descriptive	130	2,389	308	251	42
out/arm	10	descriptive	154	1,899	416	133	75
lay/hand	10	descriptive	89	1,125	181	71	101
head/bow	10	descriptive	62	1,001	120	106	39
hand/clutch	10	descriptive	9	633	53	47	11
cover/story	10	television	812	56	332	121	51
station/public	10	television	438	31	55	169	47
show/tonight	10	television	535	35	30	69	1
columnist/syndicated	10	television	465	7	89	71	16
tape/show	10	television	321	23	50	119	25

A large number of items were judged erroneously flagged by a fluent speaker. That is, the fluent speaker felt these items did have value for learners of general English. Table 3.5 below provides a sample of these items at all three parameters.

Table 3.5. A Sample of Pairs Flagged for Having Unbalanced Dispersion at All Three Parameters Judged to be Erroneously Flagged by a Fluent Speaker

Pair	Parameter	Type	Spo.	Fic.	Mag.	News.	Acad.
ago/moment	2.5	spoken	1,416	318	7	4	30
good/evening	2.5	spoken	4,592	420	42	51	12
level/significantly	2.5	academic	15	4	3	13	506
indicate/difference	2.5	academic	2	1	14	4	641
effect/significant	2.5	academic	48	6	64	54	2,487
well/obviously	5	spoken	964	72	24	28	19

afternoon/good	5	spoken	882	239	44	26	3
right/absolutely	5	spoken	1,459	134	88	76	25
back/welcome	5	spoken	5,599	185	87	169	21
important/implication	5	academic	20	1	50	7	560
think/definitely	10	spoken	619	40	78	138	11
very/strongly	10	spoken	939	34	89	135	105
question/interesting	10	spoken	630	62	109	64	243
turn/back	10	fiction	846	6,801	924	645	345
high/level	10	academic	128	17	44	47	333

In addition, many items were judged by a fluent speaker to be specialized and of little use to general learners that were not flagged at any of the three parameters. Table 3.6 below provides a sample of such items.

Table 3.6. A Sample of Pairs Judged to be of Little Use to General Learners Not Flagged for Having Unbalanced Dispersion by Any of the Three Parameters

Pair	Genre	Spo.	Fic.	Mag.	News.	Acad.
budget/congressional	political	396	1	172	318	111
baseball/bat	sports	177	308	139	153	29
bake/cookie	food	52	68	352	142	7
bond/junk	business	202	4	310	203	9
bone/marrow	medical	368	124	263	312	143

Considering a collocational pair's general value regarding its usefulness across multiple genres proved to be an important criterion; the parameters utilized and aided by manual checking identified 1,413 of the 12,615 pairs (11.2%) as not being of significant value for learners of general English. However, dispersion data alone was not sufficient in identifying unbalanced items. Often, the parameter set either was too inclusive or not inclusive enough, and thus, items would be included that were of little value or items of little value were not identified for removal. The most reliable parameter was shown to be a cut-off of 2.5% of occurrences across three or more genres. While the parameter was useful in helping to flag items to reconsider, using fluent-speaker judgments was still deemed to be necessary since the parameter could only flag 48.1% of the items of little value.

The largest group with unbalanced dispersion data was pairs occurring primarily in the academic section. While these pairs would benefit students who plan to do scientific research or read academic journals, such items may not be useful for general language needs. Thus, identifying such genre-specific, unbalanced items can be extremely valuable, either to exclude them or even focus on them if appropriate.

The same can also be said for the large number of pairs that occurred mainly in the fiction section. They consisted of language fiction writers employ to describe what the reader cannot see. Thus, these items do not often occur in any other genres. Again, their inclusion or exclusion depends on the course of study.

Biber et al. (1998) reminded us that corpora can skew the type of data we seek depending on their contents. This was evident in the disproportionate amount of collocations related to cooking found in the magazine and newspaper sections of the corpus used. Since the magazines and newspapers sourced by the COCA (Davies, 2008) regularly featured recipe articles, such items had disproportionate frequency counts. The pedagogical value of directly teaching such items to learners of general English is questionable except for those who plan to work in the food industry. Therefore, despite their high frequency, they do not have much pedagogical value for such learners.

Items mostly occurring in the spoken section were also apparently influenced by the data source. The COCA (Davies, 2008) sourced much of its spoken section data from television, particularly news or talk shows. Therefore, most items with unbalanced dispersion in the spoken section consisted of the language newscasters or talk show hosts use, such as commercial break transitions, guest introductions, etc. The value of such items for learners of general English is also arguably low, and their discovery shows the importance of dispersion data.

Also of note is how the COCA (Davies, 2008) divides its genres and the effects that it has on dispersion data. While much academic and fiction-related language was easily identified, the same cannot be said for other specialized genres, such as business-related collocations, despite it clearly being a specialized genre. Business-related terms were distributed throughout the COCA's spoken, magazine, and newspaper genres but not in particularly high-frequency counts compared to academic language, which had its own dedicated genre. Only a small portion of the spoken, magazine, and newspaper genres took data from business-related sources, such as financial magazines. If the COCA had been designed with this in mind, such language could have also been easily identified. Such data would be of clear value to learners of business English.

In summary, the data analysis showed that the most reliable parameter could identify items deemed to be of little value for learners of general English by a fluent speaker only 48.1% of the time. Therefore, concerning the extent to which dispersion data can identify useful collocations, this experiment revealed that it is limited because the best parameter could only identify about half of the items that needed to be excluded. A fluent speaker's manual analysis of the items in question is thus considered essential in addition to using such a parameter.

Is Corpus Chronological Data Reliable for Identifying High-frequency General English MWUs?

Because of the large number of collocations, researchers recommend delimiting items selected for direct study to those with the highest value for learners. If a learner's goal is to master general English, then that learner should only focus on collocations that occur in a balanced way over time. Clearly, learners should not spend time on items that are dated, too modern, or only occurred during a limited period. However, research on the usefulness of this criterion regarding identifying useful collocations has not been conducted to date. Thus, questions remain concerning its usefulness and how such a task can be accomplished. Therefore, the following experiment determined whether or not chronological data from a corpus could be relied upon to help identify MWUs most representative of high-frequency lemmatized concgrams.

In this experiment, the data source was the 12,615 lemmatized concgrams that were identified previously. Chronological data for the identified collocates was first collected from the COCA (Davies, 2008) in the same four-year sections as in the previous experiment. First, fluent speaker intuition was used to determine the best percentage cut-off. The lemma list was therefore examined using fluent speaker intuition for pairs that were either dated, too modern, or only occurred during a specific period. Very few such items existed, but the items found had approximately 5% or fewer occurrences in one or more of the four chronological sections. Just as dispersion data were analyzed, chronological data was also analyzed to find items having less than 10%, 5%, and 2.5% of total occurrences in one or more sections. Then, pairs flagged at these parameters were examined by a fluent speaker to determine if they truly were dated, too modern, or not useful because they only occurred during a specific period and thus are not worthy of direct instruction for learners of general English. Next, all remaining items in the list were also examined by a fluent speaker to determine if the parameters could not identify items that were dated, too modern, or had little value because they only occurred during a specific period. Finally, all items identified as being

Addressing Gaps in the Research 55

unbalanced by a fluent speaker were examined to determine whether they were dated, only occurred during a specific period, or were too modern. Finally, to determine the extent to which the chronological data distribution cut-offs truly identified items that were not worthy of direct instruction, the collocates were then judged by a fluent speaker regarding their usefulness.

Out of the parameters tested, all three were shown to be highly unreliable. Approximately 80% of items flagged as having unbalanced chronological data dispersion were judged to be erroneously flagged by a fluent speaker in all three parameters (see Figure 3.3 below). At 2.5%, only 15 of the 73 items (20.5%) flagged were judged to be flagged accurately. At 5%, only 28 of the 163 items (17.2%) flagged were judged to be flagged accurately. And at 10%, only 67 of the 335 items (20.0%) flagged were judged to be flagged accurately. Only five items beyond the parameters tested were judged by a fluent speaker to be of little use for learners because of chronological issues. Only 67 out of 12,615 items (0.53%) were found to have little use for learners because of chronological issues.

Figure 3.3. Percentage of Items Accurately and Erroneously Flagged for Balanced Chronological Data Distribution at all Three Parameters

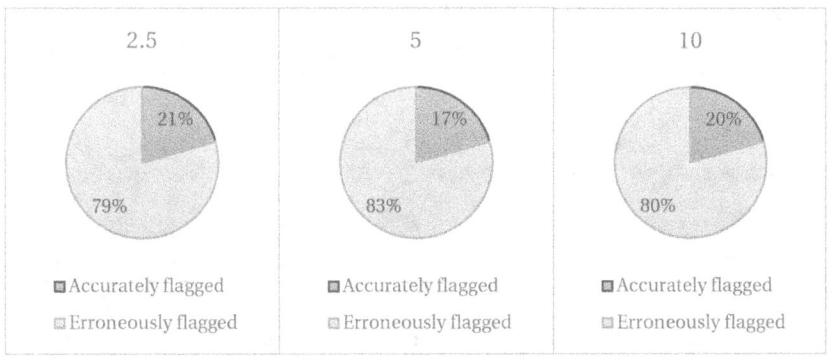

In Table 3.7 below, a sample of some of the items flagged at all three parameters as being of little value to learners of general English because of their chronological data dispersion imbalance, and the five items deemed to have chronological issues by a fluent speaker that were not flagged by any of the parameters are shown.

Table 3.7. Samples of Items Accurately Flagged at All Three Parameters (2.5, 5, and 10) and Items Judged to Have Chronological Issues Not Flagged by Any of the Parameters (X)

Pair	Parameter	1990-1994	1995-1999	2000-2004	2005-2009
marriage/gay	2.5	10	159	608	527
budget/amendment	2.5	155	445	7	7
suicide/bomber	2.5	13	103	624	615
cell/embryonic	2.5	7	24	375	401
package/stimulus	2.5	251	21	141	554
fund/hedge	5	57	294	268	797
health/reform	5	1050	241	61	939
force/coalition	5	255	27	451	281
new/millennium	5	31	387	422	123
bond/junk	5	535	99	57	32
saving/loan	10	1312	197	95	113
industry/tobacco	10	263	563	194	59
rain/acid	10	427	204	149	83
change/regime	10	63	55	371	238
word/processor	10	282	123	53	74
trade/deficit	X	424	354	121	174
federal/deficit	X	392	109	92	132
federal/insurance	X	345	84	66	139
land/reform	X	156	158	78	290
health/universal	X	169	62	95	279

Considering a collocational pair's balanced chronological data distribution, when determining its value for learners, it proved to be much less effective than the dispersion data analysis since only 0.53% of the 12,615 pairs were found to have chronological issues that would make them not worthy of direct study for learners of general English. Furthermore, each parameter was shown to be unreliable in that the vast majority of the items they flagged as having unbalanced distribution were deemed valuable for learners of general English.

Often, items erroneously flagged by the parameters were new collocations deemed by a fluent speaker to have high potential to be used regularly in the future, such as 'Internet/access.' The items accurately flagged or deemed by a fluent speaker to have chronological issues were mainly related to temporal events, such as with 'new/millennium.' Items with sudden surges in frequency counts were mainly connected to political events, wars, or similar time-sensitive events.

Some items were also deemed too modern, so their future value was unclear. For instance, 'cell/embryonic' was flagged by one of the parameters and considered by a fluent speaker to be of questionable value. It may have high-frequency counts simply because it is a new technology being discussed often, and it is unclear whether the collocation will continue to be used. Science may become commonplace or outdated; thus, the term may eventually not be discussed as often.

Only a few items were considered dated, such as 'word/processor.' Notably, the corpus only provides data back to 1990. If older data were available, then there would be more dated collocations identified. However, within the data's 19-year span, very few dated collocations were found. In addition, a more in-depth analysis would have been possible if a more detailed chronological breakdown of data was available (i.e., a breakdown by year instead of four-year sections).

This experiment demonstrated the limited efficacy of chronological data analysis. Not only were there a minimal number of items with chronological issues, but all of the parameters tested were also highly unreliable, thus again necessitating fluent speaker judgment. Therefore, this criterion was shown to be of limited value for useful collocation identification.

Is Consideration for Colligation an Important Criterion for Identifying High-frequency General English MWUs?

Three main approaches (semantic, structural, and lexical) to researching collocations exist, each with virtues and limitations. As discussed earlier, the lexical approach has advantages over the other approaches for my research on identifying collocations useful for learners of general English. However, the ability of the structural approach to consolidate data via grammatical matrices certainly has the potential to improve results. How to achieve this and the extent of the improvement are important questions to examine. Therefore, this next experiment determined whether consideration for colligation is an essential criterion for identifying MWUs most representative of high-frequency lemmatized concgrams.

This experiment utilized the list of 11,212 MWUs derived from high-frequency lemmatized concgrams remaining after items that were deemed to have unbalanced dispersion and chronological stability in the previous experiments were manually checked for and removed. Concordance data for each of the 11,212 lemmatized concgrams was collected from the COCA (Davies, 2008) to identify the MWUs most representative of them. However, my approach necessitated writing custom concordance software to identify the most common MWUs. Using available concordance software, such as Anthony's (2018) AntConc, was not an option. My research aimed to identify only MWUs where both lemmas occurred, a function not possible with AntConc or other concordance software. Furthermore, the large amount of data (over 11,000 pairs) required a batch processing option, another feature not possible with current concordance software. Therefore, the bespoke concordance software AntWordPairs (Anthony, 2013) was created specifically for my research. It utilizes Someya's (1998) E-lemma list for lemma family identification. For coding purposes, Someya's lemma list could not contain duplicate entries, and thus, I modified it to remove homonyms. The software GoTagger (Goto, 2005) was used for speech tagging. The software Textcrawler (Digital Volcano, 2011) was used for colligational marker substitution.

The first step was to collect concordance data (example sentences) for each of the 11,212 lemma pairs. Lemmatized concordance searches were conducted, using the COCA's (Davies, 2008) online concordance interface, to identify instances when the collocate occurred either three words to the left or right of the node word. The rationale for this length (seven words) was influenced by findings on typical human memory limitations (Miller, 1956). The COCA's (Davies, 2008) interface provides options for extracting 100, 200, 500, or 1,000 example sentences. Since more data provides the most reliable results, I collected 1,000 example sentences for each pair. However, because of COCA download limits and the time required for sentences to load, 1,000 sentences were deemed impractical. However, to ensure that 500 example sentences provided as reliable data as 1,000 sentences would, results from ten random lemma pairs were compared using both 500 and 1,000 example sentences. Starting with pairs with frequency counts of 1,000 or more, every 500th pair was selected from the list, which was sorted by frequency. Extracting 500 example sentences per lemma pair essentially created a mini corpus for each pair consisting of approximately 13,000 words per pair.

The next step was to identify specific categories of lexical items that occur in high-frequency that could be substituted with colligational markers. Essentially, the goal was to experiment with several items that could be substituted with a marker that does not impede the meaning of the MWU while providing more accurate frequency counts. However, since no previous research existed, several items needed to be chosen and experimented with. A MWU search was conducted on all 11,212 lemma pairs without consideration for collocation. Then, a scan of the full data by a fluent English speaker revealed that particular categories of words (pronouns) occurred quite often in the MWUs identified and could easily be substituted without disrupting the meanings of the MWUs. In addition, some other word categories were noticed and thus were used in the colligation treatment: 'months,' 'days of the week,' 'ordinal numbers,' and 'cardinal numbers.'

Adjustment for homonyms in the corpus data was necessary to use the colligational categories. This was done by part of speech tagging using GoTagger (Goto, 2005) and making replacements using Textcrawler (Digital Volcano, 2011). First, all instances of the pre-nominal possessive pronoun 'her' were changed to 'his' to not interfere with the object pronoun 'her.' Then, instances of the ordinal number 'second' were changed to 2nd to not interfere with the noun 'second.' Next, instances of the nominal possessive personal pronoun 'his' were changed to 'hers' to not interfere with the pre-nominal possessive pronoun 'his.' Then, the nominal possessive personal pronoun 'mine' was replaced with 'yours' to not interfere with the noun 'mine.' Furthermore, instances of the months 'May' and 'March' were replaced with 'January' to not interfere with the auxiliary verb 'may' and the verb 'march,' respectively. In addition, the day of the week abbreviations 'Sun,' 'Wed,' and 'Sat' were replaced with 'Mon' so as not to interfere with the noun 'sun' and the verbs 'wed' and 'sat,' respectively.

Then, Textcrawler (Digital Volcano, 2011) was used to replace all the pronouns, months, days of the week, and ordinal and cardinal numbers with distinct colligational markers in each mini-corpus. The data was then processed with AntWordPairs (Anthony, 2013) to identify the most common MWU each lemma pair occurred in. Because the resulting data was excessive, only MWUs occurring in 5% or more of the corpora were collected. The next step was to take a random sample of the MWUs affected by the colligational treatment and do a concordance search with the original data not treated for colligational issues to judge whether a different MWU was identified.

Data from ten random concordance searches were examined for differences between using 500 and 1,000 example sentences. The same top MWU was identified for every pair examined between the two amounts, regardless of whether 500 or 1,000 example sentences were used. The data also shows that the frequency counts varied very little when comparisons were made. Table 3.8 below shows the top MWU identified for each of the ten pairs examined.

Table 3.8. The Top MWU Identified When 500 and 1,000 Example Sentences Were Utilized

Lemma	POS	Lemma	POS	Multi-word Unit Identified	% (500 sentences)	% (1,000 sentences)
announce	verb	week	noun	announced last week	21.6	20.0
trade	adj.	deficit	noun	trade deficit	85.6	84.7

body	adv.	upper	adj.	upper body	87.2	86.2
up	adv.	high	adv.	high up	70.0	66.5
little	adv.	better	adv.	little better	100	97.5
court	noun	hold	verb	court held	40.2	42.5
take	verb	charge	noun	take charge	46.4	38.7
care	verb	people	noun	people who care	15.4	10.8
get	verb	look	noun	get a look	23.2	15.7
too	adv.	often	adv.	too often	57.4	33.4

After the initial concordance search, distinct categories of words were found to occur frequently in the MWUs identified. The vast majority of these were pronouns. Therefore, colligational markers were created for the following types of pronouns:

1. Pre-nominal possessive pronouns (your, his, her, their, my, our, its)

2. Subject pronouns (I, you, he, she, they, we, it)

3. Object pronouns (me, us, him, her, them)

4. Nominal possessive personal pronouns (theirs, his, hers, yours, mine)

5. Singular reflexive personal pronouns (myself, yourself, himself, herself, itself, yourselves, themselves, ourselves)

It was also determined that four additional colligational categories should be replaced with colligational markers since they were noticed in the original concordance search, did not disrupt the meaning of the MWU as a whole, and could potentially provide more accurate frequency counts. There were:

1. **Months:** (January, Jan, February, Feb, Mar, April, Apr, May, June, Jun, July, July, August, Aug, September, Sept, October, Oct, November, Nov, December, Dec)

2. **Days of the week:** (Sunday, Sun, Monday, Mon, Tuesday, Tue, Wednesday, Wed, Thursday, Thurs, Friday, Fri, Saturday, Sat)

3. **Ordinal numbers:** (1st, 2nd, 3rd, 4th, 5th, 6th, 7th, 8th, 9th, 10th, 11th, 12th, 13th, 14th, 15th, 16th, 17th, 18th, 19th, 20th, 21st, 30th, 40th, 50th, 60th, 70th, 80th, 90th, 100th, first, second, third, fourth, fifth, sixth, seventh, eighth, ninth, tenth, eleventh, twelfth, thirteenth, fourteenth, fifteenth, sixteenth, seventeenth, eighteenth, nineteenth, twentieth, twenty-first, thirtieth, fortieth, fiftieth, sixtieth, seventieth, eightieth, ninetieth, one-hundredth)

4. **Cardinal numbers:** (1, 2, 3, 4, 5, 6, 7, 8, 9, 10, 11, 12, 13, 14, 15, 16, 17, 18, 19, 20, 21, 22, 23, 24, 25, 26, 27, 28, 29, 30, 31, 32, 33, 34, 35, 36, 37, 38 ,39 ,40 ,41 ,42 ,43 ,44 ,45 ,46 ,47 ,48 ,49 , 50, 51, 52, 53, 54, 55, 56, 57, 58 , 59 , 60, 61, 62, 63, 64, 65, 66, 67, 68, 69, 70, 71, 72, 73, 74, 75, 76, 77, 78, 79, 80, 81, 82, 83, 84, 85, 86, 87, 88, 89, 90, 91, 92, 93, 94, 95, 96, 97, 98, 99, 100, 200, 300, 400, 500, 600, 700, 800, 900, 1,000, 2,000, 3,000, 4,000, 5,000, 6,000, 7,000, 8,000, 9,000, 10,000, 20,000, 30,000, 40,000, 50,000, 60,000, 70,000, 80,000, 90,000, 100,000, 200,000, 300,000, 400,000, 500,000, 600,000, 700,000, 800,000, 900,000, 1,000,000, one, two, three, four, five, six, seven, eight, nine, ten, eleven, twelve, thirteen, fourteen, fifteen, sixteen, seventeen, eighteen, nineteen, twenty, thirty, forty, fifty, sixty, seventy, eighty, ninety, one-hundred, one-thousand, ten-thousand, one-hundred thousand, one-million)

It should be noted that the items selected for colligational treatment is not an all-encompassing list, and other potentially useful colligational patterns may undoubtedly have been present in the data. However, due to practical time and computing limitations, my research only dealt with the above colligational categories and the items listed within them.

After all, mini-corpora were adjusted for homonyms and processed with AntWordPairs (Anthony, 2013) to identify the MWUs and fluent speakers extracted the MWUs most representative of how each lemma pair co-occurs, the number of MWUs identified that were affected by the colligational treatment was counted. The results are shown in Table 3.9 below.

Table 3.9. Amount of Top MWUs That Were Affected by Each of the Colligational Treatments

Colligational treatment	Number of top multi-word units affected	Percentage of total lemma pairs
Pre-nominal possessive pronouns	259	2.1%
Subject pronouns	208	1.7%

Cardinal numbers	171	1.4%
Object pronouns	74	0.6%
Ordinal numbers	14	0.1%
Singular reflexive personal pronouns	1	0.007%
Nominal possessive personal pronouns	0	0%
Months	0	0%
Days of the week	0	0%
Grand totals	727	5.8%

The colligational treatment for pre-nominal possessive pronouns was shown to be the most common. As seen in Table 3.9 above, 2.1% of the lemma pairs' top MWUs were affected by this colligational treatment. Treatments for subject pronouns and cardinal numbers also affected several items. In total, 6.4% of all the top MWUs (719 items[2]) identified were affected by all the colligational treatments conducted.

Ten random samples were then taken from the top three types of colligation treatment found to affect the top MWU identification. These were then compared to a top MWU search with untreated data. Out of the 30 items selected, only 13 (43.3%) resulted in different MWUs being identified. For items affected by the pre-nominal possessive pronoun treatment, only four out of ten top MWUs differed. With the subject pronoun treatment, only three out of ten top MWUs differed. Six out of ten top MWUs differed with the cardinal number treatment. These results are summarized in Tables 3.10, 3.11, and 3.12 below.

Table 3.10. Comparison Between Ten Random Samples of Top MWUs Affected by the Colligational Treatment for Pre-nominal Possessive Pronouns and the Results That Would Have Occurred Without the Treatment

Lemmatized concgram pair	MWU identified w/ colligational treatment	MWU identified w/o colligational treatment
hand (noun) wave (verb)	waved * hand	waved a hand
live (verb) life (noun)	live * life	live life

---

[2] Note that this total differs from the 727 colligational issues listed in Table 3.9 above. This is because eight MWUs had two colligational issues.

base (verb) experience (noun)	based on * experience	based on experience
attention (noun) focus (verb)	focus * attention	focus attention
head (noun) gun (noun)	gun to * head	gun to his head
hand (noun) extend (verb)	extended * hand	extended his hand
eye (noun) wipe (verb)	wiped * eye	wiped her eye
life (noun) ruin (verb)	ruin * life	ruin your life
put (verb) hand (noun)	put * hand	put her hand
sit (verb) desk (noun)	sitting at * desk	sitting at his desk

Note. Items in bold indicate those that showed differences in the top MWU identified, and instances of a slot in which a pre-nominal possessive pronoun exists are represented with '*.'

Table 3.11. Comparison Between Ten Samples of Top MWUs Affected by the Colligational Treatment for Subject Pronouns and the Results That Would Have Occurred Without the Treatment

Lemmatized concgram pair	MWU identified w/ colligational treatment	MWU identified w/o colligational treatment
see (verb) mirror (noun)	**mirror * saw**	**mirror and saw**
wear (verb) dress (noun)	**dress * wore**	**wearing a dress**
take (verb) back (adverb)	**take it back**	**take back**
how (adverb) interact (verb)	how * interact	how they interact
get (verb) when (adverb)	when * got	when I got
make (verb) hard (adverb)	makes * hard	makes it hard
could (verb) suppose (verb)	suppose * could	suppose you could
belong (verb) where (adverb)	where * belong	where I belong
think (verb) pretty (adverb)	think * is pretty	think she is pretty
want (verb) whenever (adverb)	whenever * want	whenever you want

Note. Items in bold indicate those that showed differences in the top MWU identified, and instances of a slot in which a subject pronoun exists are represented with '*.'

Table 3.12. Comparison Between Ten Random Samples of Top MWUs Affected by the Colligational Treatment for Cardinal Numbers and the Results That Would Have Occurred Without the Treatment

Lemmatized concgram pair	MWU identified w/ colligational treatment	MWU identified w/o colligational treatment
get (verb) second (noun)	**got * seconds**	**seconds to get**
nearly (adverb) decade (noun)	**nearly * decades**	**nearly a decade**
just (adverb) year (noun)	**just * years**	**just a few years**
live (verb) mile (noun)	**live * miles**	**live within 50 miles**
nearly (adverb) mile (noun)	**nearly * miles**	**nearly a mile**
minute (noun) second (noun)	**minutes * seconds**	**seconds to one minute**
estimate (verb) percent (noun)	estimates that * percent	estimates that 80 percent
divide (verb) group (noun)	divided into * groups	divided into two groups
over (adverb) month (noun)	over * months	over six months
roughly (adverb) percent (noun)	roughly * percent	roughly 10 percent

Note. Items in bold indicate those that showed differences in the top MWU identified, and instances of a slot in which a cardinal number exists are represented with '*.'

Regarding the amount of data collected to create each mini-corpus used, 500 example sentences were deemed as reliable as 1,000 when comparing concordance data. The example shown in Table 3.8 above demonstrates that a collection of 500 versus 1,000 example sentences for each lemma pair made no difference in identifying the most common MWU. However, collecting the data was a manual process of copying and pasting from the COCA's interface, something it was not designed for. Therefore, unnecessary data was also copied through the process, and a multi-step method of pasting into an Excel file, then copying only the sentences and pasting again into a Word file, and then finally saving the file was necessary to remove this data. Being a cumbersome, time-consuming process, corpus computer interface designers may want to consider this for future design improvements.

When the initial concordance data was examined after processing the compiled mini-corpora, various types of pronouns occurred quite often within the MWUs identified. Other categories of words, such as cardinal numbers, also frequently occurred. Therefore, such word categories became the focus of the colligation experiment. However, other categories were also experimented with because of a lack of previous research. Not all of these proved fruitful. However, the resulting data provided insight into specific types of colligation that, when addressed, can improve the reliability of MWU identification.

The colligational treatment for pre-nominal possessive pronouns was shown to be the most useful. Treatments for singular reflexive personal pronouns, nominal possessive personal pronouns, months, and days of the week were not useful; only one item was affected in the entire list by all of these treatments. At first glance, the colligational treatment was shown to be an important step in the identification of the most frequent MWUs most representative of lemmatized concgrams, in that 719 (6.4%) of the total concgrams examined had their most common MWU change. However, when a sample of the MWUs was compared to the MWUs that would have been identified without treatment for colligation, only 43.3% of the items had differing results. Therefore, while frequent counts were always improved, the treatments did not always end with a different MWU being identified.

Before the colligational treatment could be conducted, homonym interference in the data had to be dealt with. Due to the lack of dedicated software to conduct such a task, the process was complex, cumbersome, and very time-consuming. It would also be useful if software developers considered such functionality to provide ways to improve the efficacy of such data modification.

This experiment showed the results one can expect when conducting specific colligational treatments on data. It showed how 500 example sentences that contain a target pivot word and collocate are just as reliable as 1,000 example sentences. It also showed that the colligational treatment affected MWU searches for 6.4% of the lemma pairs examined. However, when a sample of these items was examined more deeply, it was found that nearly half showed no difference in the top MWU identified. While results did improve for approximately 3% of the items examined, the steps needed to achieve these improvements were extremely time-consuming and complex. Therefore, this indicates the need for a more efficient methodology for such colligation treatments. Software designers should thus consider ways to automate such time-consuming steps.

This experiment did have its limitations. Due to the lack of previous research and no standard for conducting such data analysis, choices for the types of colligation examined were subjective. Quite possibly, other types of colligation exist in the data that could also prove fruitful if treated. Therefore, more research is needed regarding other types of colligation that may improve results if treated. Despite these limitations, this experiment provided new insights into a previously unexplored area of linguistic analysis that certainly has the potential to create resources that help improve the efficacy of second language acquisition.

What Percentage of High-frequency General English MWUs is Deemed by Fluent Speakers Worthy of Expanding Beyond Their Most Frequent Exemplar?

Corpora can no doubt help improve our ability to select useful language to teach to second language learners. However, current technology does not enable researchers to use corpora alone to identify MWUs most representative of a lemma pair. While corpora and concordance software can identify MWUs and sort them by frequency, they cannot help identify MWUs that would benefit by being expanded beyond their cores. For example, corpora and concordance software can easily identify 'come to terms' as the most common MWU of the lemma pair 'come' and 'terms' but cannot help in determining whether or not to expand such an example to include other words that frequently occur beyond this core string, such as 'to come to terms' or 'to come to terms with.' The extent to which this is an issue has not been examined in previous research; thus, this important question remains unanswered. Therefore, the next experiment I conducted was to determine the percentage of MWUs deemed by fluent speakers worthy of expanding beyond their most frequent exemplar core to provide learners with useful information about how the items commonly occur formulaically.

This experiment utilized the list of 11,212 MWUs derived from high-frequency lemmatized concgrams previously identified. All concordance data collected was processed using AntWordPairs (Anthony, 2013), and the data were broken up and distributed among five fluent English-speaking university English language professors who then identified the most frequent MWU in which the lemmas co-occur. Then, these fluent speakers examined subsequent MWUs (sorted by frequency), which also contained this top MWU along with other words to its left or right, to determine if extending the MWU to the left or right of this core MWU would provide helpful information for learners.

Fluent speakers were instructed to use their intuition and experience teaching English to determine whether or not it was appropriate to extend beyond the core MWU. For instance, if the top MWU identified is 'come to terms' and the second 'come to terms with,' a fluent speaker would most likely opt to extend and add 'with' because of its high frequency of following 'come to terms.' Furthermore, fluent speakers were instructed to utilize the frequency data available. For example, if the top MWU identified was 'come to terms' and had a frequency count of 500, and the second was 'come to terms with' and had a frequency count of 499, for all practical purposes, it is clear that in such a situation it would be best to opt to have the MWU 'come to terms with' represent the lemma pair 'come' and 'terms.' After this analysis, a random sample of 100 of the final MWUs identified was examined to determine how many MWUs fluent speakers extended beyond the top MWU.

Addressing Gaps in the Research

In the random sample, fluent speakers opted to extend MWUs beyond the core pivot and collocate 53% of the time. For instance, the most frequent MWU for the lemma pair 'come' and 'term' was found to be 'come to terms' at 243 occurrences (see Table 3.13 below). However, the next most common string in the data beyond 'come to terms' was 'come to terms with' (229 occurrences), and beyond that, 'to come to terms with' (129 occurrences). Therefore, a fluent speaker judged 'to **come to terms** with' as being the MWU most representative of the lemma pair 'come' and 'term' since more than half of the occurrences of '**come to terms**' were preceded by 'to,' and nearly half of the occurrences of 'to **come to terms**' were followed by 'with.'

Table 3.13. MWUs Identified From 500 Example Sentences in Which the Lemma Pair 'Come' and 'Term' Both Occur

MWU	Occurrences in 500 sentences
come to terms	243
come to terms with	229
to **come to terms**	133
to **come to terms** with	129
coming to terms	96
coming to terms with the	86
to **come to terms** with the	44
come to terms with [pre-nominal possessive pronoun]	28
coming to terms with the	26

Concerning the value of extending MWUs beyond the core pivot and collocate, the data suggests that this is an important criterion to consider when attempting to identify MWUs most representative of lemmatized concgrams. Fluent speakers opted to extend MWUs in more than half of the items examined. Corpus data and software alone cannot add such extensions, and thus, this aspect of the study highlighted the importance of fluent speaker intuition and intervention in MWU identification.

This experiment highlighted the value of extending MWUs beyond the core MWU of a pivot and collocate. Over half of the sample examined were deemed worthy of extension beyond the most frequent MWU core by fluent speakers. However, because this procedure cannot be accomplished using software, it can be very time-consuming. Thus, more research needs to be done to determine if this process could somehow be automated.

What Percentage of MWUs Most Representative of High-frequency General English Lemmatized Concgrams Has Low Semantic Transparency?

Despite there being agreement regarding the value of collocations, even today, there is still much disagreement as to what should and shouldn't be considered a collocation. Some researchers believe that words that frequently co-occur but that are also semantically opaque should only be considered collocations (Moon, 1994; 1997; Van der Meer, 1998). This is logical because it would help delimit items to only those with a higher learning burden. However, the extent to which high-frequency collocations are semantically opaque or transparent remains to be seen. Therefore, I conducted the following experiment to determine the value of semantic transparency as a criterion for high-frequency collocation selection.

This experiment utilized the list of 11,212 MWUs derived from high-frequency lemmatized concgrams identified previously. Two English as a second language teachers analyzed the list of MWUs to determine their level of semantic transparency. Determining a collocation's level of semantic transparency is not a simple task, and it is essential to recognize that there is a cline of fixity (Kellmer, 1994; Shin, 2006). Grant and Bauer (2004) suggested distinguishing such items along this cline by breaking them down into the following four categories:

1. **Literals:** A collocation is a 'literal' if the meaning of each word alone is the same as when it is paired as a collocation (e.g., 'eat breakfast').

2. **ONCEs:** If only one word in the collocation is figurative, that collocation is considered a 'ONCE' (e.g., 'driven to quit').

3. **Figuratives:** A collocation is a 'figurative' when it is not literal, but it is possible to understand the collocation by pragmatically reinterpreting it (e.g., 'hit the nail on the head').

4. **Core idioms:** If the whole collocation is figurative, and it is impossible to reinterpret its meaning to understand it, then it is considered a 'core idiom' ('pull someone's leg').

However, while analyzing the data, the raters began noticing items that did not fit into the above categories. Therefore, a new category was created:

5. **Specials:** When collocations contained a homonym that could easily be misunderstood (when the significantly rarer homonym is used), the collocation was marked as 'special' (e.g., 'bear children'). Collocations were also given this rating when they had particular meanings that learners have a high probability of misunderstanding (e.g., 'boot camp,' 'social security,' 'foster care'). In addition, if a collocation seemed to be formed arbitrarily (when there is no rhyme or reason why a particular word is used and not another logical alternative), it was also given this rating. Examples include 'take measures,' 'deliver a speech,' and 'to stand trial.' For instance, why do we 'take measures' and not say 'create measures'? Why do we 'deliver a speech' but not 'deliver gossip'? Furthermore, wouldn't it be more logical to say 'have a trial' instead of 'stand trial'? Recognizing these 'special' arbitrary ways language combines is essential to recognizing the learning burden, and thus, this new category was added.

After the two raters analyzed all the data and gave each collocation a rating, inter-rater reliability was determined using the percent agreement measure. Inter-rater reliability was confirmed, with only 245 collocations found to have disagreement between the two raters. At 97.9%, the two raters clearly could be relied upon to rate the items similarly. Any items that there was disagreement on were re-examined and their ratings were reconsidered. Table 3.14 below is a summary of the final results.

Table 3.14. Semantic Transparency Ratings of the Collocations (Percentage of Total Items in Parenthesis)

Literal	ONCE	Figurative	Core Idiom	Special
9,641 (86%)	676 (6%)	193 (1.7%)	179 (1.6%)	519 (4.7%)

The results revealed that fluent speakers considered the vast majority of high-frequency collocations examined (86% of them) to be literal formulations. As the value of high-frequency items is well-known and other factors may influence the learning burden of these items (e.g., L1 congruency), suggesting that such a large chunk of the language not be taught directly to students as Moon (1994) did seems imprudent.

High-frequency vocabulary is ubiquitous. It can cover up to 80% or more of the running words in most texts (Nation, 2008). Therefore, Nation (2001b) stated such vocabulary deserves direct teaching time. However, how should such vocabulary be taught to learners? Actually, research indicates that learning collocations is easier than learning words in isolation (Ellis 2001). For example, Bogaards (2001) found that multi-word expressions containing familiar words were retained 10% more than completely new single words immediately after a learning session and also 12.1% more in a delayed posttest three weeks later. Therefore, it would be ideal to teach high-frequency vocabulary with their common collocates in the form of MWUs that the collocates typically occur within. However, such items would be excluded from what is to be taught directly if Moon's (1994) position that literal formulations not be considered as collocations is followed. So, if learners want to study high-frequency collocations in the most efficient way possible, semantically transparent collocations must be taught since they make up the vast majority of how high-frequency vocabulary co-occurs.

Indeed, the learning burden of a literal collocation can be low, and semantically opaque collocations deserve more focus than transparent items. However, the results of the above experiment provided evidence that shows how using a measure such as semantic transparency alone to select collocates to teach directly can be problematic in that if literal formulations are excluded from direction instruction, that would mean that most high-frequency MWUs would be excluded. Furthermore, in addition to the factor of L1 congruency, the results also showed that certain items may deserve special treatment (e.g., collocations that contain homonyms or arbitrarily formed collocations).

Therefore, the problem of utilizing rigid definitions for linguistic phenomena to achieve the practical goal of selecting items to teach second language learners was highlighted. Some potential new categories researchers should consider when rating the semantic transparency of a collocation were also revealed. With this knowledge, teachers and future researchers may be able to improve their choices concerning the explicit teaching of high-frequency collocations.

What Percentage of MWUs Most Representative of High-frequency General English Lemmatized Concgrams Has Low L1-L2 Congruency With Japanese, Chinese, and Korean?

Researchers have agreed that L1-L2 congruency is an important factor that affects a word or MWU's learning burden (Gitsaki, 1996; Laufer & Eliasson, 1993; Nesselhauf, 2005). By identifying such items, researchers can identify specific items that deserve more teaching time. However, there is still a lack of research regarding the extent to which congruency with certain L1s and high-frequency English worthy of direct instruction affects their learning burden. Therefore, to fill this gap in the research, I conducted the following experiment to determine the L1-L2 congruency of high-frequency MWUs between English and Japanese, Chinese, and Korean.

This experiment utilized the same list of 11,212 MWUs derived from high-frequency lemmatized concgrams identified previously. Translators gave L1-L2 congruency ratings to each MWU in the list. The rating was from 0-12 points, with 12 points equating to total congruency. A 12-point system was used because the vast majority of MWUs in the list consisted of either three or four words; thus, it was easy to divide this number by three or four. First, the translators counted the number of words in the MWU and divided that by 12. For instance, each word in the MWU 'wake up late' would thus be worth 4 points. Then, they compared each word in the MWU to each word in its translation. If a word's literal meaning differed or was absent in the translation, it was not awarded points. If a word was in the same word family but was a different part of speech, had a slight semantic difference, or a combination of both, the word was given half its allotted points. If the translation contains an extra word not present in English, then points allotted for one word were subtracted. If one of the English words in the MWU did not exist in the L1, such as English articles, the translators were instructed to ignore it. The translators were also instructed to ignore when there was a different word order because of the different grammar across the languages in question.

The results of the comparison between 11,212 English MWUs and their Japanese translations can be seen in Table 3.15 below. To create a resource that can be practically studied directly, choosing items with ratings of 0-6 resulted in a list of 3,415 MWUs for Japanese learners.

Table 3.15. L1-L2 Congruency Ratings of High-frequency English MWUs With Japanese Translations

Rating	0-3	4-6	7-9	10-12
	996	2,419	2,905	4,851

The results of the comparison between 11,212 English MWUs and their Chinese translations can be seen in Table 3.16 below. To create a resource that can be practically studied directly, choosing items with ratings of 0-9 resulted in a list of 2,501 MWUs for Chinese learners.

Table 3.16. L1-L2 Congruency Ratings of High-frequency English MWUs With Chinese Translations

Rating	0-3	4-6	7-9	10-12
	387	732	1,382	8,711

The results of the comparison between 11,212 English MWUs and their Korean translations can be seen in Table 3.17 below. To create a resource that can be practically studied directly, choosing items with ratings of 0-6 resulted in a list of 2,081 MWUs for Korean learners.

Table 3.17. L1-L2 Congruency Ratings of High-frequency English MWUs With Korean Translations

Rating	0-3	4-6	7-9	10-12
	997	1,084	2,907	6,224

The results made it salient that a significant percentage of the MWUs examined were not congruent with the languages compared with. The data above does show some variation between the three languages regarding the ratio of MWUs that fell into the four rating categories. Regardless, such a large number of incongruent items for all three languages compared makes it clear that L1-L2 congruency is a crucial factor to consider when choosing English items for these learner groups to focus on.

Using this criterion creates a list of items that need additional study time because of the higher learning burden of such items. In addition, such a list could also be useful for learners with limited time to study but who want to focus only on items they have a higher chance of making errors. For instance, the lists can be significantly shorter if a cut-off of 3 out of 12 points is utilized. Such a reduction in volume could be significant in helping learners achieve fluency more efficiently when they have limited study time.

However, there are limitations to the implications of its findings. Mainly, L1-L2 translation and L1-L2 congruency analysis are not exact sciences. Often, there are various ways a particular MWU can be translated, and there are differences in the quality of the translation depending on the translator's skill. In addition, there is an aspect of subjectivity in making L1-L2 congruency ratings. Furthermore, a procedure for conducting such a comparison has not been utilized in previous research, and thus, I had to create a rubric with which to judge congruency. While these limitations are acknowledged, at the same time, it should also be recognized that such issues are unavoidable due to the nature of the task. Therefore, my approach best approximated to the fullest extent possible the answer to the research questions set forth.

These experiments made salient the extent to which L1-L2 congruency affects the learning burden of high-frequency English MWUs. A significant amount of the 11,212 English MWUs examined was incongruent to an extent with the L1s in question. Thus, the learning burden of a large proportion of the items examined can be affected by the learner's L1. This large percentage warrants using L1-L2 congruency as a criterion in selecting particular items to spend additional study time on to help learners avoid making errors influenced by their L1. While there are limitations to interpreting the results, it should still be considered a good step toward improving the efficacy of second language learners acquiring collocational fluency.

Is Fluent Speaker Intuition Reliable Regarding High-frequency Vocabulary Usage in Context Creation?

Corpora, by their very nature, are not perfect. For some tasks, relying on a fluent speaker may be preferable. For instance, a fluent speaker's intuition may be more reliable when creating example sentences to help teach MWUs because they can consider the word frequencies of the context they create. Having such example sentences is key to helping students learn how a word or phrase is used in the proper context while not increasing the learning burden of the item.

However, to date, no previous large-scale research has examined the extent to which a fluent speaker's intuition can be relied upon to create example sentences with content that mostly falls into the high-frequency realm. Therefore, this next experiment I conducted examined the type of content fluent speakers create with the instructions to write example sentences for high-frequency MWUs with the aim of using high-frequency supporting context as much as possible while still producing natural, appropriate examples. This experiment was thus designed to determine whether or not fluent speakers could be relied upon using only their intuition to accomplish such a task.

This experiment utilized the same list of 11,212 MWUs derived from high-frequency lemmatized concgrams identified previously. The concgrams were distributed among four fluent speakers—two Americans and two Canadians—who wrote an example sentence for each MWU. These fluent speakers are experienced ESL practitioners with ten years or more experience teaching English as a second language. Each practitioner was instructed to choose high-frequency contextualized context whenever possible while creating natural and appropriate sentences. Essentially, the goal of the fluent speaker was to create an example sentence that did not increase the learning burden while also highlighting the MWU's typical usage in the language.

Then, the formulaic sequences alone were processed with Heatley et al.'s (2002) RANGE program to determine the extent to which the contents fell into the high-frequency realm. This program combines the BNC and COCA corpora to produce a frequency list to which other texts can be compared. This frequency list consists of the top 25,000 word families in the combined corpora, along with levels for noise in the data (26-30, 32, and 34), proper nouns (31), and compound nouns (33). After that, the same analysis was repeated, but with the formulaic sequences within the example sentences created by the fluent speakers. The results were then compared to each other. Finally, the formulaic sequences within the example sentences were processed with Cobb's (2013) Vocabprofiler to determine which of the top 3,000 word families (high-frequency vocabulary) were not covered by the data.

Example sentences written by all four fluent speakers were combined, which in total consisted of 159,211 tokens. The formulaic sequences alone and the formulaic sequences with the example sentences were examined using Heatley et al.'s (2002) RANGE. Tables 3.18 and 3.19 below show their coverage of the top 34 groups of 1,000 word families of English.

Table 3.18. Word Family Frequency Breakdown of Formulaic Phrases Using RANGE

Word Family Frequency Level	Total Tokens / %	Total Types / %	Families
1	25,081/78.04	1,942/44.28	923
2	4,445/13.83	1,202/27.41	721
3	2,071/ 6.44	811/18.49	589
4	277/ 0.86	215/ 4.90	202
5	95/ 0.30	84/ 1.92	84
6	38/ 0.12	33/ 0.75	31
7	10/ 0.03	10/ 0.23	10
8	11/ 0.03	11/ 0.25	10
9	4/ 0.01	4/ 0.09	4
10	0/ 0.00	0/ 0.00	0
11	3/ 0.01	3/ 0.07	3
12	2/ 0.01	2/ 0.05	2
13	1/ 0.00	1/ 0.02	1
14	1/ 0.00	1/ 0.02	1
15	0/ 0.00	0/ 0.00	0
16	0/ 0.00	0/ 0.00	0
17	0/ 0.00	0/ 0.00	0
18	0/ 0.00	0/ 0.00	0
19	0/ 0.00	0/ 0.00	0

20	0/ 0.00	0/ 0.00	0
21	0/ 0.00	0/ 0.00	0
22	0/ 0.00	0/ 0.00	0
23	0/ 0.00	0/ 0.00	0
24	0/ 0.00	0/ 0.00	0
25	0/ 0.00	0/ 0.00	0
26	0/ 0.00	0/ 0.00	0
27	0/ 0.00	0/ 0.00	0
28	0/ 0.00	0/ 0.00	0
29	0/ 0.00	0/ 0.00	0
30	0/ 0.00	0/ 0.00	0
31	6/ 0.02	3/ 0.07	3
32	2/ 0.01	2/ 0.05	2
33	60/ 0.19	38/ 0.87	37
34	0/ 0.00	0/ 0.00	0
Not in lists	32/ 0.10	24/ 0.55	
Totals	32,139	4,386	2,623

Table 3.19. Word Family Frequency Breakdown of Formulaic Phrases Within Example Sentences Created Using Fluent Speaker Intuition Using RANGE

Word Family Frequency Level	Total Tokens / %	Total Types / %	Families
1	136,707/85.87	2,659/33.92	985
2	13,074/ 8.21	1,959/24.99	900
3	5,271/ 3.31	1,357/17.31	785
4	1,120/ 0.70	557/ 7.10	449
5	663/ 0.42	281/ 3.58	248
6	234/ 0.15	143/ 1.82	127
7	101/ 0.06	73/ 0.93	67
8	90/ 0.06	51/ 0.65	48
9	44/ 0.03	33/ 0.42	33
10	35/ 0.02	26/ 0.33	25

11	26/ 0.02	14/ 0.18	12
12	18/ 0.01	9/ 0.11	8
13	6/ 0.00	5/ 0.06	4
14	6/ 0.00	5/ 0.06	5
15	1/ 0.00	1/ 0.01	1
16	1/ 0.00	1/ 0.01	1
17	1/ 0.00	1/ 0.01	1
18	2/ 0.00	2/ 0.03	2
19	0/ 0.00	0/ 0.00	0
20	0/ 0.00	0/ 0.00	0
21	0/ 0.00	0/ 0.00	0
22	0/ 0.00	0/ 0.00	0
23	0/ 0.00	0/ 0.00	0
24	0/ 0.00	0/ 0.00	0
25	0/ 0.00	0/ 0.00	0
26	0/ 0.00	0/ 0.00	0
27	0/ 0.00	0/ 0.00	0
28	0/ 0.00	0/ 0.00	0
29	0/ 0.00	0/ 0.00	0
30	0/ 0.00	0/ 0.00	0
31	753/ 0.47	251/ 3.20	229
32	54/ 0.03	11/ 0.14	8
33	733/ 0.46	221/ 2.82	189
34	36/ 0.02	14/ 0.18	13
Not on lists	235/ 0.15	166/ 2.12	
Totals	159,211	7,840	4,140

Tables 3.18 and 3.19 show that the phrases themselves consisted of 2,623 word families, and after the example sentences were written, there were only 1,517 word families added by the example sentences.

Table 3.20 below shows the percentage of items in the top 3,000 word families of English that were not covered by any of the words in the example sentences.

Addressing Gaps in the Research 77

Table 3.20. Vocabprofiler Breakdown of Top 3,000 Word Family Words Not Covered by Example Sentences Created Using Fluent Speaker Intuition

Word Family Frequency Level	Top 3,000 word family tokens not present in example sentences	Percentage of word family not covered
K-1 families not in input:	15	1.5%
K-2 families not in input:	100	10%
K-3 families not in input:	215	21.5%
Totals	330	11%

The results showed that experienced fluent speaker intuition could certainly be relied upon to create content mainly using high-frequency vocabulary since a large amount of the context created fell into the high-frequency realm. In fact, in comparison to the percentage of items that fell into the high-frequency realm for the formulaic phrases alone, the addition of approximately 130,000 more tokens of example sentence context only reduced the percentage of tokens in the high-frequency realm by 0.92% (see token percentages for 1,000 word family groups 1-3 in Tables 3.19 and 3.20). This copious amount of high-frequency data creation revealed that fluent speaker intuition could be relied upon to supply contextual content when the goal is to create supporting context that does not add additional learning burden to the target MWU.

The value of a small but extremely frequent amount of word families was also confirmed. The words used in the entire corpus of example sentences consisted of only 4,140 word families. This indicates that certain high-frequency words are used repeatedly even when there is a great amount of data. Therefore, the value of high-frequency vocabulary and their collocations was confirmed. Furthermore, despite adding such a copious amount of context, only 1,517 word families were added since the phrases consisted of 2,623 word families. Although it is a large database, the vocabulary load (4,140 families) should be feasible for learners to handle.

One interesting aspect was the style in which the sentences were written. All four fluent speakers wrote and used language in a subtly different style. For instance, one of the fluent speakers, an avid fiction reader, more often included sentences that included quotes of what someone said in a way typical of fiction writing. Another fluent speaker wrote more often about economic issues than the other writers. Another American writer created sentences involving gun violence more often than the others. It is certainly a possibility that this variety of fluent speakers writing sentences may have contributed to the high coverage of the top 3,000 word families of English.

Although the example sentences did cover a high percentage of the top 3,000 word families of English at 89% (see Table 3.19), why 11% was overlooked should also be discussed. Ideally, writers would have included some of the words from this 11% in the sentences to expose learners to them. By their nature, corpora can never truly represent natural language perfectly. For instance, the ease with which corpora can be compiled with written texts already in digital form increases the potential for formal language to be included more often due to the nature of written texts. Also, since Vocabprofiler utilizes word family lists partially derived from the British National Corpus, differences between British and North American English occasionally explain why these words were overlooked. A few examples were 'centimetre,' 'flavour,' 'duke,' 'lord,' and 'pub.' Furthermore, the vast majority of the words not found in the top-34 (1,000 head words) word family lists were items that the program has trouble counting, such as words with hyphens ('middle-aged,' 'x-ray,' etc.). Such items highlight weaknesses in the corpus or the software rather than weaknesses in the example sentences.

While this experiment highlighted how the intuition of experienced ESL practitioners can be relied upon to produce high-frequency contextual content, some unintended discoveries were also made. The content all four fluent speakers created had subtle differences in style and focus; thus, future research should also consider this.

What is Japanese University Students' Knowledge of MWUs Most Representative of High-frequency General English Lemmatized Concgrams?

Previous research shows that it is clear that both beginner and advanced-level second language learners throughout the world lack collocational fluency (Gitsaki, 1996; Nesselhauf, 2005). Researchers also point out specific aspects of certain collocations that give them a higher learning burden than others, such as L1-L2 congruency. However, despite a variety of evidence highlighting these issues, a reliable and comprehensive resource that identifies common, useful collocations does not exist to test learners with. My research outlined in this book created such a resource. Thus, it was used in the following experiment to confirm and, more precisely, identify the extent that learner proficiency, MWU frequency, and L1-L2 congruency affect a learner's knowledge of collocations.

This experiment utilized the list of 11,212 MWUs derived from high-frequency lemmatized concgrams, their example sentences, and each item's L1-L2 congruency data. First, the list of MWUs was sorted by frequency and then divided into five sections with an equal amount of MWUs. Then, each section was sorted by the MWU's L1-L2 congruency rating. Ten MWUs were selected from each of these five sections. An attempt was made to choose

Addressing Gaps in the Research

approximately five items for each of the L1-L2 congruency ratings (0-12). However, having an equal amount in every section was impossible because the total ratings (13 different possible scores) were not divided equally. This is because some items did not receive certain scores (none of the MWUs received a score of exactly 11, for example) and scores were not all round numbers. However, every attempt was made to make as balanced of a sample as possible (see Table 3.21 below).

Table 3.21. L1-L2 Congruency Ratings of MWUs Selected for Testing Students' Collocational Fluency

L1-L2 Congruency Rating	Number of MWUs Selected
0	5
1.5	5
2	5
4	5
4.8	3
5	2
7	2
7.2	3
8	5
10	5
10.5	2
10.8	3
12	3

Then, a C-test was created with these 50 items. Each MWU consisted of a lemmatized concgram (a pivot word and its collocate), of which each of the pairs was either a noun, verb, adjective, or adverb, along with any other words that helped form its most common MWU. Frequency data were collected for each pivot and collocate, and the less frequent word was chosen as the target word for the questions. The example sentences created by fluent English speakers in a previous experiment were then utilized to create the C-test items. However, for this test, the aim was to create contexts that used only high-frequency vocabulary. Therefore, Cobb's (2013) program Vocabprofiler was used to confirm that all words in the supporting context of each sentence (outside of the MWU being tested) were high-frequency (all words occurred within the first BNC/COCA combined 3,000 word families of English).

For example, the most common MWU representative of the lemmatized concgram 'line' and 'credit' was found to be 'a line of credit.' Since 'credit' is less frequent than 'line,' it was chosen as the target item for production. The first letter of the target item and underscore lines for the remaining missing letters were provided to avoid other possible answers. So, the following sentence was utilized:

> The bank offered a line of c _ _ _ _ _ to the company to buy some new equipment.

It should be noted that in some cases (4 of the 50 questions), two letters were provided to avoid other possibilities, and in one case, the first five letters of the word were provided. These modifications were determined after pilot tests were conducted first with seven fluent English speakers and then a group of 39 learners at the same university as those who took the final test.

The final test was then administered to Japanese university students with a wide range of proficiency. There were 549 students tested at a Japanese foreign language university campus with approximately 2,000 students. These students were also asked to provide their TOEFL scores when tested. The results were tallied and then analyzed to determine whether their TOEFL scores correlated with their ability to produce answers on the test and whether the frequency of the MWUs or L1-L2 congruency affected their knowledge of the items.

Participant TOEFL scores ranged from 310 to 677. The mean score was 421. A total of 14 outliers' data was removed from the study because these students did not get any questions correct on the test. Their average TOEFL score was 367. Hence, the new N-size became 535 with a mean TOEFL score of 421, low of 310, high of 677, and S.D. of 48.18. Cronbach's alpha reliability was $\alpha = .78$; thus, the test exhibited internal consistency. The highest score on the test was 52% correct, and the lowest was 2% correct. The average score on the test was 23% correct. Therefore, it was found that the students had very low knowledge of the test items. The analysis did not show a correlation between students' TOEFL scores and knowledge of the test items.

An analysis of the data was conducted to determine if there was a correlation between item knowledge and frequency level (see Table 3.22 below). A linear progression was not found concerning increasing frequency versus increasing correct responses across all five levels of item frequency tested. However, if one level was removed (level 2), a linear relationship was identified, which showed that as item frequency increased, so did correct responses.

Table 3.22. Mean Scores for Test Items Organized by Frequency Level

Frequency Level	M	SD	Total Correct Responses
1	0.63	0.85	338
2	1.29	1.38	689
3	0.65	0.91	350
4	1.09	0.89	583
5	2.20	1.62	1,179

Multiple regression analysis with TOEFL as the dependent variable and item frequency as the independent variable was also conducted (see Table 3.23 below). Due to the Bonferroni adjustment to control for Type II error, the p-value was set at .01 (.05 divided by five comparisons). For the multiple regression analysis, the results were $R = .57$, $R^2 = .33$, Adjusted $R^2 = .32$. For the ANOVA, the results were $F(5,529) = 51.49$, $p = .000$.

Table 3.23. Multiple Regression Analysis and Correlation Coefficient with TOEFL as the Dependent Variable and Item Frequency as the Independent Variable

Factor	B	Beta	t	p	r
Lvl 1	8.48	.15	3.44	.001*	.42
Lvl 2	3.39	.10	2.14	.032	.41
Lvl 3	9.98	.17	3.81	.000*	.44
Lvl 4	3.54	.07	1.68	.094	.27
Lvl 5	8.05	.27	5.83	.000*	.50

The R-squared value of 32% indicates that the model explained the variability of response data around its mean to an extent. It was also found that three levels of item frequency predicted TOEFL scores and that there was a significant but small correlation between item frequency levels and item score ($r = .28$). The strongest predictor was level 5. The beta weight of .27 indicated that a change in level 5 item scores of one standard deviation would increase TOEFL scores by 13 points (.27 X 48.18). While significant predictors, item frequency levels did not have particularly strong beta weights and thus cannot be construed as the most salient variable in predicting TOEFL scores for the sample population.

Regarding L1-L2 congruency as a factor in predicting TOEFL scores, multiple regression analysis was conducted with TOEFL score as the dependent variable and L1-L2 congruency as the independent variable (see Table 3.24 below). Due to the Bonferroni adjustment to control for Type II error, the p-value was set at .006 (.05 divided by nine comparisons). For the multiple regression analysis, the results were $R = .61$, $R^2 = .37$, Adjusted $R^2 = .36$. For the ANOVA, the results were $F(5,529) = 34.42$, $p = .000$.

Table 3.24. Multiple Regression Analysis and Correlation Coefficient with TOEFL Score as the Dependent Variable and L1-L2 Congruency as the Independent Variable

Factor	B	Beta	t	p	r
Cong0	11.92	.09	2.49	.013	.28
Cong1	0.39	.00	0.10	.923	.12
Cong2	14.71	.21	4.46	.000*	.50
Cong4	0.77	.02	0.51	.614	.26
Cong5	-4.93	-.05	-1.28	.200	.20
Cong7	9.20	.13	2.98	.003*	.39
Cong8	12.50	.21	5.21	.000*	.44
Cong10	6.28	.18	3.95	.000*	.46
Cong12	5.70	.08	2.00	.05	.32

The R-squared value of 36% indicates that the model explained the variability of response data around its mean to an extent. TOEFL scores were predicted by four congruency levels: Cong2, Cong7, Cong8, and Cong 10. Cong2 and Cong10 both had a standardized beta weight of .21, indicating that an increase in congruency scores by one standard deviation would result in a corresponding increase in TOEFL scores by 10 points. The results generally supported the hypothesis that L1-L2 congruence generally leads to better test scores, with a significant but very small correlation between congruency levels and overall vocabulary score ($r = .06$). However, the low beta weights do not indicate congruency between L1 and L2 phraseology as salient.

In summary, the results indicate that Japanese university students' knowledge of MWUs most representative of high-frequency lemmatized concgrams is extremely low at only 23% correct. Regarding TOEFL scores correlating with collocational knowledge, there was no correlation found. Regarding frequency and L1-L2 congruency being factors that affect the learning burden of the collocations, only a small correlation was found for both variables.

The results indicated that the students had very little knowledge of the test items, with an average score of only 23% correct. Despite the test items being a balanced selection of high-frequency collocations to which fluent speakers had no problem producing the answers, students still struggled with such questions. Even the highest score on the test (52% correct) would be considered as failing by standard measures in Japan. This is unsurprising since comprehensive resources to teach such items do not yet exist, and therefore, students were not taught such knowledge directly. Because such resources did not exist at the time, textbook writers had no resources to refer to when selecting items to focus on. Therefore, it seems as if collocations are not directly taught, resulting in a lack of collocational fluency.

The results also indicated no correlation between TOEFL scores and the test items. There are several reasons why this may be the case. First, if students had taken the TOEFL iBT test, which requires speaking and writing, and not the ITP test, then the data may have correlated because the test utilized required productive knowledge. In addition, the lack of comprehensive resources that identify high-frequency collocations could also play a role. Since no such resource existed, proficiency test creators couldn't assign load on such items.

Previous studies have shown that frequency and L1-L2 congruency increases an item's learning burden. My research, however, could not show a strong correlation between frequency and L1-L2 congruency and students' ability to provide a correct answer. This is because the students' mean scores were so low that a proper analysis was not possible. A lack of collocational fluency across the board makes extracting the data necessary to show a correlation impossible. So, frequency and L1-L2 congruency may still be factors, and further research should be conducted to help make the extent to which they are more salient. For example, a receptive knowledge test may provide data indicating a stronger correlation. Regardless, the overall lack of collocational fluency I found indicated that students, teachers, and materials writers in Japan need to focus on this aspect of vocabulary depth knowledge more.

This experiment examined Japanese university students' knowledge of high-frequency collocations. It found that their knowledge of such items was extremely low. It also found that TOEFL scores did not correlate with collocational knowledge and that there was only a small correlation between frequency and L1-L2 congruency and collocational knowledge. The students' overall lack of knowledge, even those with high TOEFL scores, limited my ability to show a correlation between frequency and L1-L2 congruency and collocational knowledge. Thus, more research is needed to determine how much of an influence these two factors truly have on a collocation's learning burden. However, this overall lack of knowledge does indicate that this is an area that needs much more focus by teachers and materials writers to help Japanese university students achieve collocational fluency in English.

Conclusion

Regarding what an ideal corpus frequency data cut-off is for identifying MWUs, one occurrence per million tokens proved optimal. It resulted in a list of 11,212 lemma pairs. This number may initially seem impractical for explicit instruction. In reality, these MWUs only consist of approximately 3,000 word families in total and have high coverage of the top 3,000 word families of English. Hence, this frequency cut-off was determined to be ideal and practical.

As far as corpus dispersion data being reliable for identifying MWUs is concerned, the experiment revealed that the type of data and methodology used was unreliable in identifying MWUs most representative of high-frequency lemmatized concgrams. Various parameters were experimented with, and their results were judged by fluent speaker intuition to either be too inclusive or too exclusive. Items that fluent speakers considered to occur across a wide variety of texts and thus had value in explicit learning were excluded by some parameters, while other parameters marked items as being balanced that fluent speakers viewed as not having value for explicit instruction. Therefore, it was determined that a combination of manual checking using fluent speaker intuition and a corpus data analysis such as the one used in this experiment, while time-consuming and subjective, was preferable to the steps taken.

Concerning whether or not corpus chronological data is reliable for identifying MWUs, the experiment I conducted revealed that the type of data and methodology used was not reliable in identifying MWUs most representative of high-frequency lemmatized concgrams. Various parameters were experimented with, and their results were judged by fluent speaker intuition to be too inclusive or too exclusive. Items that were considered by fluent speakers to be dated, only occurring during a limited period, or too modern and thus not yet established were excluded by some parameters, while other parameters marked items as having balanced chronological data distribution while fluent speakers viewed such items as not having value in explicit instruction. Just like the experiment regarding dispersion, it was determined that a combination of manual checking using fluent speaker intuition and a corpus data analysis such as the one used in this experiment, while time-consuming and subjective, was preferable compared to the steps taken in this experiment.

Regarding whether or not a consideration for colligation is an important criterion for identifying MWUs, the experiment's results led to several revelations. First, consideration for colligation can improve the results of MWU identification. However, the number of items improved in the current study was a very small percentage. In addition, no dedicated software existed, and thus, a very complex and time-consuming methodology was required. Hence, while colligation can sometimes be an issue, it is not necessarily a significant one for the study I conducted. This experiment also revealed that methodological and software improvements are necessary for analyzing data for colligation.

As to what percentage of MWUs was deemed by fluent speakers worthy of expanding beyond their most frequent exemplar to provide learners with useful information about how the items commonly occur formulaically, the experiment highlighted the value of extending MWUs beyond the core pivot and collocate since over half of the items examined were deemed to be worthy of expanding beyond their most frequent exemplar. While very time-consuming since it must be done manually and a technological solution did not exist, this type of data analysis was still deemed an essential step in a study such as this.

Regarding the percentage of MWUs most representative of high-frequency lemmatized concgrams that have low semantic transparency, only 14% of the items examined were considered to be either semi-figurative, figurative, a core idiom, or had features that prevented them from easily being understood (such as when a much less common homonym is part of the MWU). These results contrast sharply with how some researchers insist that literal collocations not be taught explicitly. The vast majority (86%) of the general English MWUs of high-frequency vocabulary that I identified were literal. Thus, if they were excluded from direct instruction, learners would not get the necessary exposure to master such important items. Therefore, these results highlight a new perspective on how high-frequency vocabulary collocates and what should be considered worthy of explicit instruction.

As for what percentage of MWUs most representative of high-frequency lemmatized concgrams have low L1-L2 congruency, 56.4% of the items examined in this experiment were deemed incongruent to an extent with Japanese. For Chinese, 28.5% were deemed to be incongruent to an extent. For Korean, 38.3% were deemed to be incongruent to an extent. These high percentages of incongruent items highlight the importance of conducting L1-L2 congruency analysis. Such items deserve extra teaching time; with such knowledge, learners can avoid typical errors resulting from their L1 influence.

Concerning whether or not fluent speaker intuition is reliable regarding high-frequency vocabulary usage in context creation, the experiment revealed that it was very reliable. Fluent speakers wrote nearly 160,000 tokens of content to create an example sentence for each of the 11,212 MWUs. An analysis of the added content revealed that it not only covered the vast majority of the top 3,000 word families of English (90%), but 97.39% of the words in the sentences also fell within these top 3,000 families. Therefore, it was affirmed that fluent speaker intuition can be relied upon for such a task, even on a large scale.

Concerning what Japanese university students' knowledge of MWUs most representative of high-frequency lemmatized concgrams is, the experiment conducted found that their knowledge of such items was extremely low. It was also found that TOEFL scores did not correlate with collocational knowledge and that there was only a small correlation between the factors of frequency and L1-L2 congruency and collocational knowledge. Since previous research indicated that L1-L2 congruency should affect collocational knowledge, these results contradict such findings. However, it is possible that because knowledge of the test items was so low, the effect of L1-L2 congruency was not even registering in the data. Similarly, one would expect a student's collocational knowledge to increase as their proficiency (as measured by TOEFL) increases. However, my research did not show such a correlation either. Again, it is possible that because knowledge of the test items was so low, such a correlation could not be found in the data. It also may be possible that TOEFL results do not reflect collocational knowledge. So, more research needs to be done concerning these two points.

Chapter 4

Implications and Applications

The journey to answer the questions outlined in this book led to many discoveries, methodologies being developed, resource creation, and the rethinking of theories. The questions my research explored were not only answered, but issues that were not yet salient when this research began were also revealed. The path to answering the research questions led to the development of methodologies that had not existed that future researchers can now use to confirm the results further and possibly also make additional discoveries in the field. Moreover, some answers revealed that certain methodologies did not produce valuable results compared to the time invested in them. This information can also be used by future researchers to possibly avoid wasting time on tasks that do not produce fruitful results.

The research I conducted also resulted in new questions being posed. For example, the discoveries made have the potential to lead other researchers to reconsider what should and should not be considered a collocation and what difficulties identifying such items entails. These contributions to the general theory of word co-occurrence could also prove valuable for researchers when thinking in more general terms about what language is and how it should be best taught.

Several unexpected discoveries were also made over the years as my research progressed down the path to addressing the gaps in the literature. First, as I conducted the literature review, I noted that numerous researchers pointed out how answering such questions would benefit learners but how such questions had yet to be answered. However, when the experiments were undertaken, it became clear why this was the case. The research questions could not be answered without help from numerous volunteers to accomplish many of the very time-consuming tasks. In addition to simple but time-consuming data collection and analysis, there was also a need for highly trained translators. It was challenging to put together such a team of volunteers and keep them motivated to continue the work for many years. Therefore, it became clear that this was work that one researcher could not do alone. However, because I was able to bring together a team of volunteers who were able to contribute their time and expertise, the goals were accomplished to the best extent possible under practical limitations. This is also useful information for future researchers because there are still many unanswered questions, and to answer them will probably require a similar collaborative effort.

My research on collocations also began with some assumptions that did not prove true. I initially believed a methodology that analyzed the dispersion and chronological data available from the COCA to help identify only items with balanced distribution could be created. However, despite utilizing a variety of parameters, all proved unreliable in achieving the goal set forth. Therefore, manual checking using fluent speaker intuition was relied upon instead. This was not expected and added a significant amount of work to the study. Furthermore, the need for an analysis of the dispersion breakdown of the COCA and how that possibly could be improved upon became clear. There were also some other discoveries regarding the makeup of the COCA itself. For example, a large amount of recipe-related language in certain sections of the corpus was not expected, and thus, steps needed to be taken to deal with such issues.

In addition, the realization that the vast majority of the MWUs were judged to be semantically transparent was also an interesting discovery. There was an expectation that there would be more semi-figurative and figurative formulations, but in reality, the way that high-frequency vocabulary collocates was found to mostly be in literal formulations.

A satisfying discovery was the reliability of fluent speaker intuition. Certain tasks in my research required the use of fluent speaker intuition for judgment and also for content creation. The ability of fluent speakers to utilize high-frequency vocabulary when creating example sentences for each of the MWUs identified ended up being more reliable than expected since the very large amount of added content via the example sentences they created only ended up having approximately 1% of the vocabulary being outside of what is considered to be high-frequency. This discovery has the potential for various implications for future research, and not just for research regarding collocations.

Another positive discovery was the word family breakdown of the final resource. When the findings of my research were discussed with other researchers and teachers, a similar reaction occurred when it was mentioned that approximately 11,000 MWUs were identified that should be taught explicitly. For these researchers and teachers, this volume is impractical for direct instruction. However, when it was pointed out that these 11,000 MWUs only consist of only approximately 3,000 word families, they realized that learning such items was feasible. In fact, it is not the equivalent of studying 11,000 new items. Instead, it is studying how 3,000 different words combine in various ways. For instance, 'run faster,' 'take a walk,' and 'moved away from' all occur in the list. If a learner masters these items at one point in a list, and later is exposed to 'walk from,' 'run away,' and 'move fast,' they are not learning any new lemma whatsoever. Viewing the resource from this perspective makes it possible to realize that the learning burden is not impractical.

Implications and Applications

Researchers agree about the value of high-frequency vocabulary and learning how they collocate for achieving second language fluency, but a large, comprehensive (but not dictionary-like) resource had yet to have been created. My research aimed to create such a resource (particularly custom-tailored resources for Japanese, Chinese, and Korean learners). Early on in the research, it was clear why such resources did not exist yet. Not only was the work so extensive and time-consuming, but methodologies that identified the way language naturally co-occurs also did not yet exist for each of the steps that needed to be taken. Furthermore, some methodologies already existed but needed to be improved upon.

Early on in my research, it became evident that new methodologies were going to be needed. Researchers have been talking about collocations and their importance for many years, but only in recent years has technology and theories been improved to the point where researchers have begun to talk less about collocations and more about concgrams. In fact, no other study that aimed to identify high-frequency collocations had taken a similar approach to mine (regarding the methodology of identifying collocational exemplars of lemmatized concgrams), so it was not a surprise to discover that several new methodologies needed to be invented.

To achieve my goal, I needed to determine how much data is necessary when trying to identify the MWU most representative of a lemmatized concgram. My research showed that 500 instances of co-occurrence produced similar results to 1,000 instances. Next, there was the development of a methodology to grapple with colligational issues. However, no research existed that gave guidance as to which words should be searched for and replaced with colligational markers. Examining the data showed that certain categories seemed to benefit from such a procedure, such as pronouns, months, days of the week, ordinal numbers, and cardinal numbers. Unfortunately, dedicated software to replace such words with colligational markers did not exist and thus I utilized multiple different software that had such capability when used in combination. In the end, after a very complex methodology was created, this task was achieved, albeit with results of marginal value.

After this was accomplished, additional steps needed to be taken to delimit items identified to only those with high value for students to learn. For example, in the past, researchers have utilized specific criteria, such as dispersion, to help identify only the most useful items for students to learn. However, to date, no research has examined chronological collocation data. Certainly, it will not be beneficial for students to learn either very dated collocations, collocations only occurring within a short time frame (trend-like or time-sensitive, event-related occurrences), or collocations that are yet to be established (new items that occur in high-frequency but have yet to be confirmed as permanent parts of the language). Therefore, a methodology was created to examine such corpus data to determine whether or not this criterion could improve the resource as a whole. While this methodology did identify some items that were not of value, they were only a small percentage of the total items examined.

Furthermore, it was determined that, even though a variety of parameters were experimented with, corpus data analysis itself was not found to be useful. Often, the parameters would either be too inclusive (flagging valuable items to learn as having unbalanced chronological distribution) or not inclusive enough (not flagging items with unbalanced chronological distribution). So, it was determined that a manual examination using fluent speaker intuition was essential. Even with this, the number of items identified was so small that it may not be worth the effort if the study was as large-scale as mine was.

In addition, software that could identify the MWU most representative of a lemmatized concgram in the manner I needed also did not exist. Concordance software did exist, and such a task can be done with it, but not without significant amounts of noise that would be very time-consuming to remove. For example, suppose a mini-corpus that contains 500 instances of co-occurrence of the lemma 'take' and 'walk' is examined with currently available concordance software. In that case, the first most common MWU identified will not be 'take a walk' (the most common MWU these lemmas occur in), but rather 'of the,' 'and the,' and so on. Only after much of this kind of noise in the data will instances where 'take' and 'walk' co-occur in MWUs be identified. Thus, software was needed that could focus only on searching for MWUs that only contained both lemmas. This was a complex task because I was not just searching for 'take' and 'walk,' but rather searching for either 'take,' 'took,' 'taking,' or 'takes' co-occurs with either 'walk' or 'walks.' It was quite clear that professional software development assistance was needed. Waseda University's Professor Laurence Anthony, the author of AntConc (Anthony, 2018), was contacted, and the discussion of how such a complex task could be achieved began. After a year of collaborative planning, software development, and testing, such software was finally created: AntWordPairs (Anthony, 2013). A comprehensive lemma list was needed to create this software. Such a list existed but needed to be modified to deal with homonyms because such instances would prevent the software from functioning properly. Then, the software also needed to be able to process files in bulk because I had to examine over 11,000 files of lemmatized concgrams, and processing these 11,000 files one by one would be too time-consuming. Some technical barriers were discovered and traversed, and in the end, the software was created, and the MWUs were finally identified. Such software is now available upon request from Professor Anthony.

However, technological solutions were not the only way my work on collocations contributed to new methodologies. It was discovered that there are limits to what could be achieved using technology, and if quality results that could practically be used for teaching is the goal, fluent speakers manually analyzing the data was found to be essential. This was realized when the MWUs identified by the software were examined. Often, the most frequent MWU occurring was not the best choice for teaching, and an extension of it was ideal. For example, the MWU 'come to terms' was identified as the top MWU occurring for the lemma pair 'come' and 'term' at 243 out of 500 instances. However, second in rank was 'come to terms with' at 229 out of 500 instances. When fluent speaker intuition is relied upon, it is clear that in such instances, it is preferable to extend the core top MWU by adding 'with.' In fact, this methodology proved extremely fruitful in that fluent speakers opted to do this for more than half of the items examined.

However, it should be recognized that a subjective element is introduced into the data analysis when fluent speaker intuition is relied upon. So, the question arose of whether or not this could be relied upon as a methodology. My research revealed that the answer to that question was, to a practical extent, yes. I aimed to create a resource that could be used to teach high-frequency collocations. However, just teaching the exemplary MWU that lemmatized concgrams occur in is insufficient for achieving this goal. Providing a full example sentence to help students learn the limitations and appropriateness of using these items is also important. Therefore, an example sentence was created for each of the approximately 11,000 MWUs identified. Care must be taken when creating such supporting context in that the context should not increase the learning burden. In other words, the context added should not contain vocabulary of a higher learning burden than those within the MWU itself. Ideally, all supporting contexts should be high-frequency vocabulary. So, this led to the question of whether or not fluent speaker intuition could be relied upon to create such context. Despite adding over 130,000 words of context by the fluent speakers in my study, the number of words that could be considered as 'high-frequency' (words within the top 3,000 word families) was very high at 98.2%. Therefore, it was confirmed that such a methodology was very reliable.

Furthermore, it should be noted that despite the use of the COCA (Davies, 2008), which is considered to be a large corpus in comparison to previous research done using other corpora, there were still instances of weaknesses in the data that computer analysis could not grapple with, thus again highlighting the need for manual checking of data. For high-frequency collocation selection, Ackermann and Chen (2013) also found a manual checking and vetting of items necessary in addition to what results their corpus data analysis could produce. A corpus itself contains natural language, but it is not a mirror reflection of language as a whole. The corpus compiler may attempt to include data from as wide of resources as possible to create as balanced a representation of the language as possible. Still, it will never unequivocally emulate natural language. Therefore, noise in the data is inevitable, and my research highlighted the types of noise that can appear and the extent to which it can affect the quality of any resource derived from such data.

Overall, the results point to the COCA as a very useful resource with very minor flaws. For example, language related to recipes had higher than expected frequency counts in the corpus because it sourced its data from certain magazines that often contain recipes. Recipes tend to have certain language, such as the collocates 'cup' and 'sugar,' that repeat more often than they truly occur in everyday language. So, if one simply relies solely upon corpus data, then, depending on the research's goal, results can be atypical compared to natural language. Therefore, this points to the importance of a methodology including manual data checking to deal with such weaknesses.

Another example of how my previous research contributed to a methodology can be seen in the experiment concerning semantic transparency. Researchers agree that semantic transparency affects a collocation's learning burden. Therefore, when collocations are examined, they can be broken down into categories such as literals, semi-figuratives, figuratives, and core idioms. One step in my research was to examine the nature of high-frequency lemmatized concgrams and determine their percentage in each semantic category. However, when the items were examined to place them into one of these four categories, some items did not seem to fit. A new outlier category was thus created for items that did not meet the criteria to be placed in the other categories. For example, when a MWU contained a homonym that could be easily misunderstood (when the significantly rarer homonym is used), such as 'bear' in 'bear children,' such items were put into this outlier category.

Collocations were also put into this outlier category when they had very specific meanings that learners have a high probability of misunderstanding (e.g., 'boot camp,' 'social security,' 'foster care'). In addition, if a collocation seemed to be formed arbitrarily (there is no rhyme or reason why a particular word is used despite there being more logical alternatives), it was also put into this outlier category. Examples include 'take measures,' 'deliver a speech,' and 'to stand trial.' For instance, why do we say 'take measures' and not 'create measures'? Why do we 'deliver a speech' but not 'deliver gossip'? Would it not be more logical just to say 'have a trial' instead of 'stand trial'? Recognizing these arbitrary ways language combines is essential to recognizing the learning burden. Therefore, by examining the items for this criterion of semantic transparency, the potential for a new category was discovered. Certainly, more

Implications and Applications 93

research needs to be conducted on this concept, but regardless, this discovery can improve future research.

Yet another methodology that resulted from my research was concerning L1-L2 congruency. Researchers agree that L1-L2 congruency affects a word or phrase's learning burden. One-to-one congruency equates to a lower learning burden, while when a word or phrase is said differently between two languages, such items will be much more challenging to learn. Additional time needs to be spent on such items because of this higher learning burden, and by identifying them, teachers can focus on them to help students avoid errors, such as in production (direct translation from the student's L1). However, despite researchers being aware of this issue, no methodology to specifically compare and rate L1-L2 congruency between the Japanese, Chinese, and Korean translations of the English MWUs and deal with all the particular differences between these languages existed when this current study began. A point scale was created, which gave each word in a MWU a certain score. Several issues arose that also needed to be dealt with. For instance, when linguistic phenomenon did not exist in the L1 (for example, English articles 'a' and 'the' do not exist in Japanese), such words were not included in the rating.

Furthermore, a point system had to be devised when a word and its translation were in the same word family but a different part of speech. Similarly, a rule was created for words with only slight semantic differences. Many other rules were also created to deal with various issues that arise when such a complex comparison of languages is conducted. These steps highlight the complexity of conducting L1-L2 congruency analysis since other languages will undoubtedly have other differences that must be dealt with in particular ways. Therefore, this first step towards a methodology for conducting L1-L2 congruency analysis should be considered a useful contribution to the field.

As mentioned earlier, a large-scale (but still having the potential to be explicitly taught) resource containing high-frequency collocations of general English did not exist, and therefore, creating several new methodologies was necessary. These methodologies led to fruitful results in that the resulting resources have the potential to be of high value to learners and practitioners of ESL. In general, the core English version of the list has value for learners across the globe. There are Japanese, Chinese, and Korean translations of all MWUs and example sentences from my study, but translations and further L1-L2 analysis could be conducted for any language. Therefore, this resource could be considered as just beginning its development for students across the globe rather than being considered complete. Further testing with more second-language students of varying ages across the globe is indeed called for. In fact, I co-supervised the Ph.D. work of Maryam Barghamadi at Flinders

University, who replicated my Ph.D. thesis to a good extent to produce a similar resource for Persian-speaking learners.

These resources also have a high potential to be used as a reference when creating other materials, such as textbooks or educational software. The reality is that most textbooks still focus on teaching isolated vocabulary, which is quite an inefficient and unnatural way to learn a language. Yes, collocations and MWUs exist in textbooks, but these books often do not bring students' attention to them (Gitsaki, 1996) or are not introduced systematically. Previous research has shown that when learners' attention is not brought to them, they cannot notice collocations. Hence, textbooks need to point them out. However, materials writers have lacked a reference resource when choosing such items. For many years, materials writers have relied upon comprehensive high-frequency vocabulary lists. However, until now, they have not had access to a resource that identified the MWUs most representative of how high-frequency vocabulary collocate, such as what my research created.

In addition, these resources also have the potential for direct study/explicit instruction. Just as students have studied word lists in the past, they can now study such words with their collocates within MWUs. Although some have dismissed rote learning and L1 contrastive analysis as a relic of the past, more and more researchers have now reconsidered their value because of their ability to improve upon the efficacy of learning (Avery & Baker, 1997; Hopkins & Bean, 1999; Rodriguez & Sadoski, 2000). Therefore, with the existence of this resource along with L1 translations, such study is now possible for three particular learner groups: Japanese, Chinese, and Korean-speaking learners of English.

Answering the research questions explored in this book led to the creation of major resources for Japanese, Chinese, and Korean-speaking English learners, which had not existed but have been called for by researchers for several years. These resources can potentially be used to improve the efficacy of second language acquisition by utilizing them for direct instruction or materials development. Many questions remain, such as what the best way to study such materials is. Despite this, the first step toward creating and utilizing such resources in the classroom has at least been taken. It still needs to be acknowledged that these resources and the methodologies used to create them can be improved due to the many novel steps taken to achieve this study's goals. However, at least practitioners and researchers in the field have something to work with and some data and an approach to compare to.

My research thus far has also led to many realizations regarding the theoretical knowledge of understanding collocations that were not salient before. First, the results pointed to the lexical approach toward identifying collocations as being the most useful for my research goals. My research combined this approach and some aspects of the structural approach to deal with colligation. However, these steps only proved useful to a small extent. While certain items were improved upon, the numbers paled in comparison to those that did not benefit from such a treatment. Therefore, the data points to the lexical approach being the most advantageous. When it is used, it is then possible to begin to think of language in a very different way. To again quote Lewis (1993), language "consists of grammaticalized lexis, not lexicalized grammar" (p. vi). In other words, lexis organizes language, not grammar. However, the improvements made through the colligational treatment make it clear that black-and-white condemnations or acceptance of one theory or the other is inappropriate. In fact, the structural, semantic, and lexical approaches are valid, and it simply depends on the study's goal when choosing an approach. For my research, using the lexical approach and some minor support from the structural approach proved to be the most appropriate.

In more general terms, my research thus far has contributed to the theory of collocations by helping define what is or is not a collocation for my study's goal. Just as with the approach one takes toward understanding collocations, there are a variety of equally valid definitions of what a collocation is, with some being more inclusive than others. However, from the perspective of ESL practitioners and learners, and with the very practical goal of identifying which frequently co-occurring language features should be taught explicitly to help learners attain second language fluency, my research came to some particular revealing conclusions.

Specifically, when the way high-frequency vocabulary collocate is examined and the MWUs most representative of such collocations are identified, it becomes evident that the vast majority of such items are literal formulations. However, many researchers do not consider such formulations collocations and do not believe they deserve explicit instruction because semi-figurative, figurative, and idiomatic formulations have a much higher learning burden. There is nothing wrong with such a view in that it is a logical and appropriate view of a particular linguistic phenomenon. However, my research aimed not to describe or define linguistic phenomena in rigid ways. Rather, the goal was to identify how high-frequency vocabulary co-occurs to help learners master how to use it properly and, in turn, attain fluency in that area of second language proficiency. So, the real question is not what is or is not a collocation but rather what commonly co-occurring language needs to be taught.

For example, if the approach of not accepting any literal formulations to be collocations is taken, as researchers such as Moon (1994; 1997) believed, it can be problematic in that there is a significant loss to the volume of high-frequency collocations since only a minority of the items I identified were non-literal formulations. The idea that a learner could gain 'collocational fluency' by simply mastering the 1,000 or so non-literal formulations is unfeasible since mastering such knowledge often takes learners a lifetime. In fact, some researchers have already pointed out that fluent speakers can have upwards of hundreds of thousands of collocations in their lexicons. In addition to this issue, there is another to consider: L1 congruency. For example, when a literal formulation is excluded as being considered a collocation but that formulation is incongruent with the learner's L1, the learner will have a high probability of making an error with such an item. When they try to produce the formulation, they may directly translate how it is said, word for word, from their L1 and thus create an unnatural formulation. In other words, they will make an error. The task of instructors is to help students avoid errors and to help them produce appropriate language. Therefore, there is a need to focus on creating resources that help students attain collocational fluency rather than putting limits on what can be provided because of rigid linguistic phenomena definitions. My research has helped make it salient that this theoretical flexibility is essential to conduct such an applied linguistic research approach as my research utilized.

Considering the concepts mentioned above, it becomes clear that understanding how to fill the gaps in the research I aimed for is more about perspective. From the perspective of 'what needs to be taught' rather than 'what falls into a rigid categorization of collocations,' one begins to think very differently about collocations and how to develop such fluency in second language learners. Answering the research questions explored thus led to the creation of major resources for Japanese, Chinese, and Korean-speaking English learners, which to date had not existed but have been called for by researchers for many years. These resources can potentially be used to improve the efficacy of second language acquisition by utilizing them for direct instruction or materials development.

After completing the study on identifying high-frequency collocations and creating resources for Japanese, Chinese, and Korean learners, I have expanded this research methodology to tackle academic English MWUs. I led a team of researchers who created a similar large-scale MWU resource for learners of academic English (Rogers et al., 2021). L1-L2 congruency analysis was conducted with Japanese; thus, the nearly 5,000 MWUs the resulting resource contains should be of high value for Japanese learners. This resource is available as a study smartphone app called Academic English Phrases. The contents are also used in a Microsoft Word real-time academic English auto-suggest plug-in called Academic English Auto-Suggest. Both of these resources were created and made available for free due to a Japanese government 'Grant-in-Aid for Scientific Research' (KAKENHI), 基盤研究(C)（一般）Project Number 21K00775. The success of this project showed the potential of my methodology to be applied to different genres of

English. Thus, future research could be possible for other genres, such as business and medical English.

Many questions remain, though, such as verifying the results of my research, discovering the best way to study such materials, and conducting L1-L2 congruency with other languages, of which many speakers study English (e.g., Spanish speakers from Latin America). Despite this, the first step toward creating and utilizing such resources in the classroom has at least been taken. These resources and the methodologies used to create them can, of course, be improved upon. However, at least practitioners and researchers in the field now have something to work with, some data, and an approach to utilize or verify.

I will now discuss a real-world application of one of the resources conducted so far. The Japanese MWU resource that resulted from the research described in this book became part of the official curriculum of my faculty at the university where I am employed and has been for eight years. Studying the resource's contents is required for English language majors for the first two years of their study within a required English communication course as supplementary study to the course's textbook (the course's primary focus). Students have to study 500 MWUs per semester for four semesters. They have weekly quizzes on each set of 50 MWUs they study, and there are also questions on the course's final test from all the MWUs they studied over the semester.

The contents are presented to students in a Leitner-algorithm spaced-repetition smartphone application (app) named 英語マスター3千 [English Master 3,000] (Rogers, 2016). I developed and released the contents within this app because studying with apps that use a Leitner-based algorithm can be more efficient than the traditional paper-based method. For example, Goodwin-Jones (2010) explained how the computer's ability to space the intervals between when items are shown can help them commit those items to their long-term memory more efficiently than studying those items from paper lists. Yamagata et al. (2022) agreed about the advantage of spaced repetition. A Leitner algorithm-based spaced repetition has been stated to have even further advantages compared to simple time-based spaced repetition (Rogers, 2014). This is because not only are items shown to learners over time-based intervals, but the users can mark items as difficult or easy, and in turn, difficult items will come back to be studied more often while items marked as easy will be shown less. Rogers and Reid (2015) experimented with such a Leitner algorithm-based app. After students studied with the app, the average test results were 57% correct, while studying the same number of similar items on paper resulted in an average of 41% correct.

Rogers (2017b) reported the results of the first semester of the app's usage at the university. Over the semester, 134 students took 810 quizzes. The results of the quiz scores were remarkably high, with an average of 90.2%. Regarding any correlations with other metrics, the top ten students who had the most minutes spent studying with the app also made the most significant gains in their TOEIC score after the semester (see Table 4.1 below). There is thus a positive correlation between TOEIC gains and minutes studied in that seven out of ten students had significantly more minutes than the average (202 minutes) of all minutes studied by students.

Table 4.1. Top Ten TOEIC Gains in Comparison to Minutes Studied with the App

Student ID	TOEIC Gain	Minutes Studied
1	160	592
2	200	590
3	150	388
4	210	372
5	150	344
6	230	323
7	150	310
8	160	199
9	225	164
10	180	155

Total TOEIC scores did not correlate with the minutes studied, though. Some students with high TOEIC scores stated that the app's contents were easy for them and they didn't need to study it. Data indicates this to be true in that the top 20 students' TOEIC scores predicted high app cumulative scores, with 18 out of 20 students receiving passing grades.

The first year's trial was judged to be a success by the faculty and after that, adopted as an official part of the required curriculum. As of today, the app has been studied for over eight years by approximately 1,000 students at the university, and these students have studied the contents of the app for over 14,000 hours. The app is also available to the general public. As of 2023, it has been downloaded approximately 4,000 times with 134,000 user sessions to date on the Apple App Store and has approximately 53,000 downloads on the

Google Play Store. Google does not provide 'session' data, so this data cannot be provided. In addition, similar smartphone apps were also released for Chinese (Rogers, 2017c) and Korean learners (Rogers, 2017d).

Chapter 5

Conclusion

As mentioned previously, although the research I conducted thus far has several clear limitations on how its results can be interpreted, used, and relied upon, it should still serve as an excellent first step towards achieving the goal of helping learners master collocational fluency. The overarching approach taken to achieve the goals of this research was post-positivism. In other words, steps were taken to answer the questions that approximated reality while acknowledging unavoidable weaknesses.

For example, high-frequency vocabulary lists such as Nation's (2004) BNC 3,000 or West's (1953) GSL are useful resources that have been used to achieve practical learning goals for years. However, some of the words in the lists can undoubtedly be improved upon. In addition, one could also argue from certain perspectives that some of the vocabulary that is excluded that ranked between entries 3,001 to 3,100 are more useful than items that ranked from 2,900 to 3,000 in Nation's list. However, that is beyond the point. There is a variety of perspectives that one can take to approach such a goal, and all are valid. Still, when there is a need for some sort of resource to fill a gap in research, some decisions must be made that make the results unavoidably limited in their, for lack of a better term, 'validity.' As I progressed along the journey of solving the research questions outlined in my research, I found more and more that the key to solving the task at hand was to avoid harsh black-and-white thinking, admit that results will never be unequivocal, and make the best approximation possible within unavoidable constraints.

With that said, some specific limitations should be acknowledged when interpreting the results of this work thus far. First, just as Nation (2001) said that setting a frequency cut-off is unavoidably arbitrary for creating a high-frequency vocabulary list, the same was true for my research. There certainly are useful collocations that occur less than the one occurrence per million token cut-off that my research utilized. With this in mind, my resources are not comprehensive, unequivocal lists. Furthermore, it can also be true that this frequency cut-off may be too inclusive and thus identify items that may not have the most value for explicit study. If a small-scale study was done, the data could be more precise. However, because of the scale of my research, this unavoidable frequency cut-off reliability limitation needs to be acknowledged.

In addition, although the bulk of my research has been quantitative, I realized that corpus data could not be solely relied upon to produce results that agree with fluent speaker intuition. So, it was necessary to include somewhat subjective judgments by fluent speakers to help achieve my study's goals. This included judgments as to which MWUs should be considered useful across a wide variety of topics (balanced dispersion), which were chronologically stable, which MWUs would be improved upon if their MWU core was extended, and regarding the semantic transparency of the MWUs examined. Furthermore, unavoidably subjective judgments were also made when conducting L1-L2 congruency analysis. This is in addition to translating nearly 160,000 words of content into three languages. Translation is not an exact science since there are a variety of ways that something can be translated. However, the translation teams did their best to examine the example sentences, determine the meaning conveyed by the MWUs, and translate them into the best equivalents possible. L1-L2 congruency analysis is not an exact science, though. In fact, I had to create an original methodology just to conduct it. It should be noted, however, that due to the extremely time-consuming process necessary and the difficulty in finding volunteers qualified enough to analyze the data for this criterion on such a large scale, how the results of my research can be interpreted has clear limitations since there was no reliability confirmation done on the translations. Unfortunately, this was not practically possible; thus, more work should be done concerning this in the future. However, it should be noted that all translators who participated in this study were professionals.

Moreover, my finding concerning students' knowledge of the items was also limited to Japanese university students. Therefore, learners from different L1s, levels of education, or backgrounds may have varying results if tested the same way. So, more research is indeed called for in this regard. Furthermore, I only tested productive knowledge. There certainly could be different results found if receptive knowledge was tested. Hence, more research needs to be done to determine the extent to which learners know such items.

Furthermore, this assumes these items are important and worthy of study. That has yet to be determined. However, Rogers (2017b) did find correlations between the study time of the resources created for Japanese learners and the TOEIC gains those students made. Whether or not causation exists remains to be seen, but this is still evidence pointing in the direction of the contents being of value for learners. Moreover, the fact that the resource was adopted as an official part of the Japanese university's required course curriculum and utilized for over eight years by approximately 1,000 students at the university is also indicative of the resource's value.

However, much work still needs to be done to determine the best way to teach the items identified. The first steps of identifying the items and trialing a study method have been taken. Therefore, future research should further examine the best way to teach such items. Whether or not studying the items in an isolated way or with full example sentences, within larger reading passages, or whether or not learners should study more than one MWU connected to a core lemma within it ('political activists,' 'political parties,' 'political leaders') are all questions that remain unanswered. The usefulness of the smartphone app created also needs further confirmation.

It is also important to note that my research thus far does not try to refute or profess any particular belief. It was simply an exercise attempting to identify certain items worthy of explicit instruction to improve collocational fluency. It laid out a methodology and showed the results of that methodology. If practitioners find value in these results and use them, that is a bonus. However, again, my research merely laid out a methodology that could be used to achieve the goals it set forth. One should note that the phrase 'could be used' is used and not 'should be used.' Data was provided to support why certain decisions and methodologies were taken, but I do not claim that other methods could not produce better results. My research simply showed that these are the results when these particular steps are taken. So, there is still a need for future research to be conducted regarding the approaches taken in my research.

As discussed above, various limitations in my research thus far leave the door open to several future research questions that should be answered. Hopefully, more research will be done that either builds upon what was accomplished in the studies I have conducted thus far or refutes its findings, proving that a more efficient way to accomplish the task is possible.

First, L1-L2 contrastive analysis has been done on my general English MWU list with Japanese, Chinese, and Korean. In fact, if ideal materials could be created, there would be translations of these contents and L1-L2 contrastive analysis conducted for all learner L1s. However, this is a tremendous amount of work, so researchers and translators will need to collaborate in the future if this is ever to be achieved. In particular, it would be extremely useful for Spanish-speaking English learners if L1-L2 contrastive analysis could be conducted in Spanish. Large Spanish-speaking immigrant groups in countries such as the United States could benefit greatly from the results of such research.

Also, as discussed in previous sections, some technological limitations existed, creating the need to use software not designed for the tasks. This less-than-ideal approach led to very complex and time-consuming methodologies. Therefore, future research should inquire how software could be improved upon, such as for dealing with colligational issues. It would be ideal if software existed that could easily and accurately part-of-speech tag certain categories of words that could be easily counted together.

Furthermore, several steps in my research had to be conducted manually. If technological solutions existed, a significant amount of time could be saved, and more accurate work could be done. Corpus compilers should note the difficulty in accessing and analyzing dispersion and chronological data to identify items that fluent speakers consider unbalanced. Concordance software developers could also note the necessity for manually extending MWUs beyond their cores and possibly discover automated solutions.

Clearly, much research still needs to be conducted before we can further improve the efficacy of obtaining collocational fluency. It is hoped that future researchers, materials writers, translators, software developers, and ESL practitioners collaborate more to enable the community to answer these difficult questions in the most expedient way possible. Ideally, learners would receive an answer to these questions as soon as possible, and it is our job and duty as educators to provide them with what they need to help them achieve their learning goals. This book outlined my efforts to achieve this important overarching goal.

References

Ackermann, K., & Chen, Y. (2013). Developing the academic collocation list (ACL) - A corpus-driven and expert-judged approach. *Journal of English for Academic Purposes, 12*(4), 235-247.

Aghbar, A. (1990, October). *Fixed expressions in written texts: Implications for assessing writing sophistication* [Paper presentation]. Meeting of the English Association of Pennsylvania State System Universities, United States.

Al-Zahrani, M. (1998). *Knowledge of English lexical collocations among male Saudi college students majoring in English at a Saudi university* [Unpublished doctoral dissertation]. University of Pennsylvania.

Alexander, R. (1984). Fixed expressions in English: Reference books and the teacher. *ELT Journal, 38*(2), 127-134.

Almela, M., & Sanchez, A. (2007). Words as "lexical units" in learning/teaching vocabulary. *International Journal of English Studies, 7*(2), 21-40.

Anthony, L. (2013). *AntWordPairs (Version 1.0.2)* [Computer software]. Waseda University. http://www.antlab.sci.waseda.ac.jp/

Anthony, L. (2018). *AntConc (Version 3.5.8)* [Computer software]. Waseda University. http://www.antlab.sci.waseda.ac.jp/

Arabski, J. (1979). *Errors as indicators of the development of interlanguage.* Uniwersytet Slaski.

Avery, P., & Baker, J. (1997). Mapping learning at the secondary level. *Clearing House, 70*(5), 279-285.

Bahns, J., & Eldaw, M. (1993). Should we teach ESL students collocations? *System, 21*(1), 101-114.

Barghamadi, Rogers, J., Arciuli, J., Han, W., & Muller A. (2023). L1-L2 congruency as a criterion to identify collocations based on contrastive analysis. *Australian Journal of Applied Linguistics, 6*(1), 1-14.

Bartan, O. S. (2019). Lexical collocation errors in literary translation. *Dil Dergisi, 1*(170), 73-88.

Bauer, L., & Nation, P. (1993). Word families. *International Journal of Lexicography, 6*(4), 253-279.

Biber, D., Conrad, S., & Cortes, V. (2004). If you look at...: Lexical bundles in university teaching and textbooks. *Applied Linguistics, 25*(3), 371-405.

Biber, D., Conrad, S., & Reppen, R. (1998). *Corpus linguistics: Investigating language structure and use.* Cambridge University Press.

Biber, D., Johansson, S., Leech, G., Conrad, S., & Finegan, E. (1999). *Longman grammar of spoken and written English.* Pearson Education.

Biskup, D. (1992). L1 influence on learners' renderings of English collocations: A Polish/German empirical study. In P. Arnaud & H. Bejoint (Eds.), *Vocabulary and Applied Linguistics* (pp. 1-12). Macmillan.

Boers, F., Eyckmans, J., Kappel, J., Stengers, H., & Demecheleer, M. (2006). Formulaic sequences and perceived oral proficiency: Putting a lexical approach to the test. *Language Teaching Research, 10,* 245-261.

Bogaards, P. (2001). Lexical units and the learning of foreign language vocabulary. *Studies in Second Language Acquisition, 23*, 321-343.

Bolinger, D. (1968). *Aspects of language.* Harcourt Brace Jovanovich, Inc.

Bolinger, D. (1976). Meaning and memory. *Forum Linguisticum, 1*(1), 1-14.

British National Corpus (1994). http://www.natcorp.ox.ac.uk/corpus/index.xml

Byrd, P., & Coxhead, A. (2010). 'On the other hand': Lexical bundles in academic writing and in the teaching of EAP. *University of Sydney Papers in TESOL, 5*, 31-64.

Channell, J. (1981). Applying semantic theory to vocabulary teaching. *English Language Teaching Journal, 35*,115-122.

Chan, T., & Liou, H. (2005). Online verb-noun collocation instruction with the support of a bilingual concordancer. *Selected Papers From the Fourteenth International Symposium on English Teaching* (pp. 270-281). Crane Publishing Co., Ltd.

Chen, P. (2002). *A corpus-based study of the collocational errors in the writings of the EFL learners in Taiwan* [Unpublished master's thesis]. National Taiwan Normal University.

Cheng, W., Greaves, C., & Warren, M. (2006). From n-gram to skipgram to concgram. *International Journal of Corpus Linguistics, 11*(4), 411-433.

Chomsky, N. (1957). *Syntactic structures.* Mouton and Company.

Chon, Y., & Shin, D. (2009). Collocations in L2 writing and rater's perceived writing proficiency. *Korean Journal of Applied Linguistics, 25*(1), 101-129.

Cobb, T. (2013). *VocabProfiler VP Compleat BNC-COCA-25.* https://www.lextutor.ca/vp/comp/

Conklin, K., & Schmitt, N. (2008). Formulaic sequences: Are they processed more quickly than nonformulaic language by native and nonnative speakers? *Applied Linguistics, 29*, 72-89.

Conzett, J. (2000). Integrating collocation into a reading and writing course. In M. Lewis (Ed.), *Teaching collocation: Further developments in the lexical approach* (pp. 70-86). Language Teaching Publications.

Cowan, L. (1989). *Towards a definition of collocation* [Unpublished master's thesis]. Concordia University.

Cowie, A. (1978). The place of illustrative material and collocations in the design of a learner's dictionary. In P. Strevens (Ed.), *In honour of A.S. Hornby* (pp. 127-139). Oxford University Press.

Cowie, A. (Ed.). (1998). *Phraseology: theory, analysis, and applications.* Oxford University Press.

Davies, M. (2008). *The corpus of contemporary American English: 425 million words, 1990-present.* http://corpus.byu.edu/coca/

Davies, M. (2010). *Word list plus collocates.* http://www.wordfrequency.info/purchase1.asp?i=c5a

Daulton, F. (2008). *Japan's built-in lexicon of English-based loanwords.* Multilingual Matters Ltd.

Davoudi, M., & Behshad, A. (2015). Collocational use: a contrastive analysis of strategies used by Iranian EFL learners. *Theory and Practice in Language Studies, 5*(12), 2646-2652.

Dechert, H. (1983). How a story is done in a second language. In C. Faerch & G. Kasper, (Eds.), *Strategies in interlanguage communication* (pp. 175-195). Longman.

Dechert, H., & Lennon, P. (1989). Collocational blends of advanced second language learners: A preliminary analysis. In W. Olesky (Ed.), *Contrastive pragmatic* (pp. 131-168). Benjamins.

DeCock, S., Granger, S., Leech, G. and McEnery, T. (1998). An automated approach to the phrasicon of EFL learners. In S. Granger (Ed.), *Learner English on computer* (pp. 67-79). Longman.

Doughty, C., & Williams, J. (1998). Pedagogical choices in focus on form. In C. Doughty & J. Williams (Eds.), *Focus on form in classroom second language acquisition* (pp. 197-262). CUP.

Du, L., Elgort, I., & Siyanova-Chanturia, A. (2021). Cross-language influences in the processing of multiword expressions: From a first language to second and back. *Frontiers in Psychology, 12*(666520), 1-18.

Durrant, P. (2009). Investigating the viability of a collocation list for students of English for academic purposes. *Journal of English for Specific Purposes, 28*(3), 157-179.

Durrant, P., & Schmitt, N. (2009). To what extent do native and non-native writers make use of collocations? *International Review of Applied Linguistics, 47*, 157-177.

Ellis, N. (2001). Memory for language. In P. Robinson (Ed.), *Cognition and second language instruction* (pp. 33-68). Cambridge University Press.

Ellis, R. (1985). *Understanding second language acquisition*. Oxford University Press.

Ellis, R. (1994). *The study of second language acquisition*. Oxford University Press.

Eriksson, A. (2012). Pedagogical perspectives on bundles: Teaching bundles to doctoral students in biochemistry. In J. Thomas & A. Boulton (Eds.), *Input, process and product: Developments in teaching and language corpora* (pp. 195-211). Masaryk University Press.

Fayez-Hussein, R. (1990) Collocations: The missing link in vocabulary acquisition amongst EFL learners. In J. Fisiak (Ed.), *Papers and studies in contrastive linguistic: The Polish English contrastive project, 26* (pp. 123-126). Adam Mickiewicz University.

Firth, J. (1957). A synopsis of linguistic theory. 1930-1955. In F. Palmer (Ed.), *Selected papers of J.R. Firth 1952-59* (pp. 168-205). Longman.

Francis, G. (1993). A corpus-driven approach to grammar: Principles, methods and examples. In M. Baker, G. Francis, & E. Tognini-Bonelli (Eds.), *Text and technology: In honour of John Sinclair* (pp. 137-156). John Benjamins.

Furukawa, J., Ford, B., Ayson, E., Cambra, K., Takahashi, L., & Yoshina, K. (1998, January 17). *Effects of a cognitive processing strategy on spelling, definitions, and reading* [Conference presentation]. The 20th Annual Conference of the Hawaii Educational Research Association. Honolulu, HI, United States.

Gairns, R., & Redman, S. (1986). *Working with words. A guide to teaching and learning vocabulary*. Cambridge University Press.

Gasser, M. (1990). Connectionism and universals of second language acquisition. *Studies in Second Language Acquisition, 12,* 179-199.

Gitsaki, C. (1996). *The development of ESL collocational knowledge* [Unpublished doctoral dissertation]. University of Queensland.

Goodwin-Jones, R. (2010). Emerging technologies. From memory palaces to spacing algorithms: Approaches to second-language vocabulary learning. *Language Learning and Technology, 14*(2), 4-11.

Goto, K. (2005). *GoTagger (Version 0.7)* [Computer software]. http://web4u.set sunan.ac.jp/Website /GoTagger.htm#

Granger, S. (1998). Prefabricated patterns in advanced EFL writing: Collocations and formulae. In A. P. Cowie (Ed.), *Phraseology, theory, analysis and applications* (pp. 145-160). Clarendon.

Grant, L., & Bauer, L. (2004). Criteria for re-defining idioms: Are we barking up the wrong tree? *Applied Linguistics 25*(1), 38-61.

Gries, S. (2008). Dispersions and adjusted frequencies in corpora. *International Journal of Corpus Linguistics 13*(4), 403-437.

Grucza, B., & Jaruzelska, H. (1978). Typowe bledy popelnanie przez kandydatow jezyku niemieckim: bledy gramatyczne i leksykalne. In F. Grucza (Ed.), *Z problematyki bledow obcojezycznych* (pp. 124-143). WSP.

Gyllstad, H. (2005). Words that go together well: developing test formats for measuring learner knowledge of English collocations. *International Journal of English Studies 7*(2), 127-157.

Hadley, A. (2001). *Teaching language in context.* Heinle and Heinle.

Halliday, M., & Sinclair, J. (1966). Beginning the study of lexis. In C. Bazell, J. Catford, M. Halliday, & R. Robins (Eds.), *In memory of J.R. Firth* (pp. 410-430). Longman.

Hausmann, F. (1984). Wortschatzlernen ist Kollokationslernen. Zum Lshren und Lernen franzosischer Wortverbindungen. *Praxis des neusprachlichen Unterrichts, 31,* 395-406.

Heatley, A., Nation, P., & Coxhead, A. (2002). *RANGE program* [Computer software]. http://www.victoria.ac.nz/lals/staff/paul-nation

Hill, J. (2000). Revising priorities: from grammatical failure to collocational success. In M.

Lewis (Ed.), *Teaching collocation: Further developments in the lexical approach* (pp. 47-67). Language Teaching Publications.

Hill, J., Lewis, M., & Lewis, M. (2000). Classroom strategies, activities, and exercises. In M. Lewis (Ed.), *Teaching Collocation: Further developments in the lexical approach* (pp. 88-116). Language Teaching Publications.

Hoey, M. (2005). *Lexical priming: A new theory of words and language.* Routledge.

Hoey, M. (1991). *Patterns of lexis in text.* Oxford University Press.

Hopkins, G., & Bean, T. (1999). Vocabulary learning with the verbal-visual word association strategy in a native American community. *Journal of Adolescent and Adult Literacy, 42,* 274-281.

Howarth, P. (1996). *Phraseology in English academic writing: Some implications for language learning and dictionary making.* Niemeyer.

Hsu, J. (2002). *Development of collocational proficiency in a workshop on English for general business purposes for Taiwanese college students* [Unpublished doctoral dissertation]. Indiana University of Pennsylvania.

Hsu, J., & Chiu, C. (2008). Lexical collocations and their relations to speaking proficiency of college EFL learners in Taiwan. *The Asian EFL Journal Quarterly, 10*(1), 181-204.

Hsu, L. (2005). *The effect of lexical collocation instruction on Taiwanese college EFL learners' listening comprehension* [Unpublished master's thesis]. National Kaohsiung First University of Science and Technology.

Huang, L. (2001). Knowledge of English collocations: An analysis of Taiwanese EFL learners. In C. Luke & B. Rubrecht (Eds.), *Texas papers in foreign language acquisition: Selected proceedings from the Texas foreign language education conference* (pp. 113-132). Texas University.

Hunston, S. (2002). *Corpora in applied linguistics*. Cambridge University Press.

Hwang, K., & Nation, P. (1995). Where would general service vocabulary stop and special purposes vocabulary begin? *System 23*(1), 35-41.

Jaen, M. (2007). A corpus-driven design of a test for assessing the ESL collocational competence of university students. *International Journal of English Studies, 7*(2), 127-147.

Jiang, N., & Nekrasova, T. (2007). The processing of formulaic sequences by second language speakers. *Modern Language Journal, 91*(3), 357-377.

Jones, S., & Sinclair, J.M. (1974). English lexical collocations: a study in computational linguistics. *Catiers de Lexicologie, 23*(2), 15-61.

Kallkvist, M. (1998). Lexical infelicity in English: The case of nouns and verbs. In K. Haastrup & A. Viberg (Eds.), *Perspectives on lexical acquisition in a second language* (pp. 149-174). Lund University Press.

Kennedy, G. (1990). Collocations: Where grammar and vocabulary teaching meet. In S. Anivan (Ed.), *Language teaching methodology for the nineties* (pp. 215-229). Regional Language Centre.

Keshavarz, M., & Salimi, H. (2007). Collocational competence and cloze test performance: a study of Iranian EFL learners. *International Journal of Applied Linguistics, 17*(1), 81-92.

Kilgarriff, A., Atkins, S. & Rundell, M. (2007, July). *BNC design model past its sell-by* [Paper presentation]. University of Birmingham 4th Corpus Linguistics Conference, Birmingham, United Kingdom.

Kjellmer, G. (1984). Some thoughts on collocational distinctiveness. In J. Aarts & W. Meijs (Eds.), *Computer corpora in English language research* (pp. 163-171). Norwegian Computing Centre for the Humanities.

Kjellmer, G. (1987). Aspects of English collocations. In W. Meijs (Ed.), *Corpus linguistics and beyond* (pp. 133-140). Rodopi.

Kjellmer, G. (1990). Patterns of collocability. In J. Aarts & W. Meijs (Eds.), *Theory and practice in corpus linguistics* (pp. 163-178). Rodopi.

Kjellmer, G. (1994). *A dictionary of English collocations*. Oxford University Press.

Korosadowicz-Struzynska, M. (1980). Word collocations in FL vocabulary instruction. *Studia Anglica Posnaniensia, 12*, 109-120.

Koya, T. (2004). Collocation research based on corpora collected from secondary school textbooks in Japan and in the UK. *Dialogue, 3*, 7-18.

Kuiper, K. (1996). *Smooth talkers*. Lawrence Erlbaum.

Larsen-Freeman, D., & Long, M. (1991). *An introduction to second language acquisition research*. Longman.

Laufer, B. (1988). *Ease and difficulty in vocabulary learning: some teaching implications* [Paper presentation]. The 22nd Annual Meeting of the International Association of Teachers of English as a Foreign Language, Edinburgh, Scotland.

Laufer, B. (1990). Ease and difficulty in vocabulary learning: Some teaching implications. *Foreign Language Annals, 23*(2), 147-155.

Laufer, B., & Eliasson, S. (1993). What causes avoidance in L2 learning: L1-L2 difference, L1-L2 similarity, or L2 complexity? *Studies in Second Language Acquisition, 15*(1), 35-48.

Laufer, B., & Girsai, N. (2008). Form-focused instruction in second language vocabulary learning: A case for contrastive analysis and translation. *Applied Linguistics, 29*(4), 694-716.

Lennon, P. (1996). Getting "easy" verbs wrong at the advanced level. *International Review of Applied Linguistics, 34*, 23-36.

Lesniewska, J., & Witalisz, E. (2007). Cross-linguistic influences on L2 and L1 collocations. *EUROSLA Yearbook, 7*, 27-48.

Lewis, M. (1993). *The lexical approach: The state of ELT and a way forward*. Language Teaching Publications.

Lewis, M. (2000a). Language in the lexical approach. In M. Lewis (Ed.), *Teaching collocation: Further developments in the lexical approach* (pp. 8-10). Language Teaching Publications.

Lewis, M. (2000b). There is nothing as practical as a good theory. In M. Lewis (Ed.), *Teaching collocation: Further developments in the lexical approach* (pp. 10-27). Language Teaching Publications.

Lien, H. (2003). *The effect of collocation instruction on the reading comprehension of Taiwanese college students* [Unpublished doctoral dissertation]. Indiana University of Pennsylvania.

Light, R. (1971). Measures of response agreement for qualitative data: Some generalizations and alternatives. *Psychological Bulletin, 76*(5), 365-377.

Lei, L., & Liu, D. (2018). The academic English collocation list. A corpus driven study. *International Journal of Corpus Linguistics, 23*, 216-243.

Lin, W., Hsiao-Ching, Y., & Ho-Ping, F. (2003). English vocabulary knowledge of first-year university students: Vocabulary size and collocational knowledge. *The proceedings of the 2003 conference and workshop on FEFL and applied linguistics* (pp. 202-213). Crane Publishing Co.

Liu, C. (1999). A study of Chinese Culture University's freshmen's collocational competence: "Knowledge" as an example. *Hwa Kang Journal of English Language and Literature, 5*, 81-99.

Liu, L. (2002). *A corpus-based lexical semantic investigation of verb-noun miscollocations in Taiwan learner's English* [Unpublished master's thesis]. Tamkang University.

Liu, E., & Shaw, P. (2001). Investigating learner vocabulary: A possible approach to looking at EFL/ESL learners' qualitative knowledge of the word. *International Review of Applied Linguistics, 39*, 171-194.

Lorenz, G. (1999). *Adjective intensification – learners versus native speakers: A corpus study of argumentative writing*. Rodopi.

Macis, M., & Schmitt, N. (2017). The figurative and polysemous nature of collocations and their place in ELT. *ELT Journal, 71*, 50-59.

Macis, M., Sonbul, S., & Alharbi, R. (2021). The effect of spacing on incidental and deliberate learning of L2 collocations. *System, 103*, 102649.

Mackin, R. (1978). On collocations: Words shall be known by the company they keep. In P. Strevens (Ed.), *In honour of A. S. Hornby* (pp. 149-165). Oxford University Press.

Martinez, R. (2013). A framework for the inclusion of multi-word expressions in ELT. *ELT Journal 67*(2), 184-198.

Marton, W. (1977). Foreign vocabulary learning as problem no. 1 of language teaching at the advanced level. *Interlanguage Studies Bulletin, 2*(1), 33-57.

Meijs, W. (1992). Inferences and lexical relations. In G. Leitner (Ed.), *New directions in English language corpora: Methodology, results, software developments* (pp. 123-152). Mouton de Gruyter.

Miller, G. (1956). The magical number seven, plus or minus two: Some limits on our capacity for processing information. *Psychological Review, 63*, 81-97.

Mitchell, T. (1971). Linguistic 'goings on': Collocations and the other lexical matters arising on the syntagmatic record. *Archivum Linguisticum, 2*, 35-69.

Monbukagakusho (2003). *The government guidelines for teaching in Japan.* www.mext.go.jp/b_m enu/houdou/11/03/990302a/990302p.htm

Moon, R. (1994). The analysis of fixed expressions in text. In M. Coulthard (Ed.), A*dvances in written text analysis,* (pp. 117-135). Routledge.

Moon, R. (1997). Vocabulary Connections: Multi-Words Items in English. In N. Schmitt & M. McCarthy, (Eds.), V*ocabulary: Description, acquisition and pedagogy* (pp. 40-63). CUP.

Morley, J. (2015). *The academic phrasebank: An academic writing resource for students and researchers.* The University of Manchester I3 Limited.

Murphy, J. (1983, March). *Words: What goes with what?* [Paper presentation]. The 17th Annual Convention of Teachers of English to Speakers of Other Languages, Toronto, Ontario.

Myers, J., & Chang, S. (2009). A multiple-strategy-based approach to word and collocation acquisition. *International Review of Applied Linguistics, 47*, 179-207.

Nation, P. (2001a). How many high frequency words are there in English? In M. Gill, A.W. Johnson, L.M. Koski, R.D. Sell, & B. Wårvik (Eds.), *Language, learning and literature: Studies presented to Håkan Ringbom* (pp. 167-181). English Department Publications 4, Åbo Akademi University.

Nation, P. (2001b). *Learning vocabulary in another language.* Cambridge University Press.

Nation, P. (2004). A study of the most frequent word families in the British National Corpus. In P. Bogaards & B. Laufer (Eds.), *Vocabulary in a second language: Selection, acquisition, and testing* (pp. 3-13). John Benjamins.

Nation, P. (2008). *Teaching vocabulary: Strategies and techniques.* Heinle.

Nation, P. & Meara, P. (2002). Vocabulary. In N. Schmitt (Ed.), *An introduction to applied linguistics* (pp. 35-54). Edward Arnold.

Nation, P., & Webb, S. (2011). *Researching and analyzing vocabulary*. Heinle.

Nattinger, J., & DeCarrico, J. (1992). *Lexical phrases and language learning*. Oxford University Press.

Nelson, F., & Kucera, H. (1979). *The Brown corpus: A standard corpus of present-day edited American English*. Brown University.

Nesselhauf, N. (2003). The use of collocations by advanced learners of English and some implications for teaching. *Applied Linguistics, 24*(2), 233-242.

Nesselhauf, N. (2005). *Collocations in a learner corpus*. John Benjamins.

Noel, J. (1992). Collocation and bilingual text. In G. Leitner (Ed.), *New directions in English language corpora: Methodology, results, software developments* (pp. 345-357). Mouton de Gruyter.

Özdem-Ertürk, Z. (2021). *Factors affecting and productive knowledge of collocations of tertiary level learners of English in Turkey* [Unpublished doctoral dissertation]. University of Hacettepe University.

Pawley, A., & Syder, F. (1983). Two puzzles for linguistic theory. In J. Richards & R. Schmidt (Eds.), *Language and communication* (pp. 191-226). Longman.

Peters, E. (2016). The learning burden of collocations: The role of interlexical and intralexical factors. *Language Teaching Research, 20*(1), 113-138.

Renouf, A., & Sinclair, J. (1991). Collocational frameworks in English. In K. Aijmer & B. Altenberg (Eds.), *English corpus linguistics* (pp. 128-143). Longman.

Ringbom, H. (1998). Vocabulary frequencies in advanced learner English: A cross-linguistic approach. In S. Granger (Ed.), *Learner English on computer* (pp. 41-52). Longman.

Robins, R. H. (1967). *A short history of linguistics*. Longman.

Rogers, J. (2013). How many high-frequency words of English do Japanese university freshmen 'know'? *Kansai Gaikokugo University Journal of Inquiry and Research, 97*, 237-252.

Rogers, J. (2016). *Eigo masutaa 3 zen*英語マスター3千. Apple and Google Play App Stores.

Rogers, J. (2017a). *What are the collocational exemplars of high-frequency English vocabulary? On identifying multi-word units most representative of high-frequency lemmatized concgrams* [Unpublished doctoral dissertation]. University of Southern Queensland.

Rogers, J. (2017b). On the implementation of a smartphone-based English app study program. *The Proceedings for the Meijo University First International Forum*, 71-76.

Rogers, J. (2017c). *Tōngyòng yīngyǔ dàshī* 通用英语大师. Apple and Google Play App Stores.

Rogers, J. (2017d). *General English for Koreans*. Apple and Google Play App Stores.

Rogers, J., Muller, A., Daulton, F., Dickinson, P., Florescu, C., Reid, G., & Stoeckel, T. (2021). The creation and application of a large-scale corpus-based academic multi-word unit list. *English for Specific Purposes, 62*(4), 142-157.

Rodriguez, M., & Sadoski, M. (2000). Effects of rote, context, keyword, and context/keyword methods on retention of vocabulary in EFL classrooms. *Language Learning 50*(2), 385-412.

Rudzka, B., Channell, J., Putseys, Y., & Ostyn, P. (1981). *The word you need: Teacher's book*. Macmillan.

Saville-Troike, M. (1984). What really matters in second language learning for academic achievement? *TESOL Quarterly, 18*(2), 199-217.

Schmitt, N. (1997). Vocabulary learning strategies. In N. Schmitt & M. McCarthy (Eds.), *Vocabulary: Description, acquisition and pedagogy* (pp. 1-46). Cambridge University Press.

Schmitt, N., & Meara, P. (1997). Researching vocabulary through a word knowledge framework: Word associations and verbal suffixes. *Studies in Second Language Acquisition, 19*, 17-36.

Shin, D. (2006). *A collocation inventory for beginners* [Unpublished doctoral dissertation]. Victoria University of Wellington.

Simpson, R., & Mendis, D. (2003). A corpus-based study of idioms in academic speech. *TESOL Quarterly, 37*(3), 419-441

Sinclair, J. (1991). *Corpus, concordance, collocation*. Oxford University Press.

Sokmen, A. (1997). Current trends in teaching second language vocabulary. In N. Schmitt & M. McCarthy (Eds.), *Vocabulary: description, acquisition and pedagogy*. Cambridge University Press.

Someya, Y. (1998). *E-lemma list*. https://lexically.net/downloads/BNC_word lists/e_lemma.txt

Skinner, B. (1957). *Verbal behavior*. Appleton-Century-Crofts.

Stubbs, M. (1995). Collocations and semantic profiles: On the cause of the trouble with quantitative methods. *Function of Language 2*(1), 1-33.

Taylor, C. (1983). Vocabulary for education in English. *World Language English, 2*(2), 100-104.

Tseng, F. (2002). *A study of the effects of collocation instruction on the collocational competence of senior high school students in Taiwan* [Unpublished master's thesis]. National Taiwan Normal University.

Twaddell, F. (1973). Vocabulary expansion in the TESOL classroom. *TESOL Quarterly, 7*(1), 61-78.

Underwood, G., Schmitt, N., & Galpin, A. (2004). The eyes have it: An eye-movement study into the processing of formulaic sequences. In N. Schmitt (Ed.), *Formulaic sequences*. John Benjamins.

University Centre for Computer Corpus Research on Language. (n.d.) *CLAWS7 tag set*. http://ucrel.lancs.ac.uk/claws7tags.html

van der Meer, A. (1998). Collocations as one particular type of conventional word combinations, their definition and character. *EURALEX '98, 1*, 313-322.

Wang, C. (2001). *A study of the English collocational competence of English majors in Taiwan* [Unpublished master's thesis]. Fu Jen Catholic University.

Webb, S., & Nation, P. (2008). Evaluating the vocabulary load of written text. *TESOLANZ Journal, 16*, 1-10.

Wilkins, D. (1972). *The learner's vocabulary for text analysis*. Lensing Verlag.

Wilks, Y. (2005, June-July). REVEAL: The notion of anomalous texts in a very large corpus. *Tuscan Word Centre International Workshop*, Certosa di Pontignano, Tuscany, Italy.

Wood, D. (2004). An empirical investigation into the facilitating role of automatized lexical phrases in second language fluency development. *Journal of Language and Learning, 2*(1), 27-50.

Woolard, G. (2000). Collocation – encouraging learner independence. In M. Lewis (Ed.), *Teaching collocation: Further developments in the lexical approach* (pp. 28-46). Language Teaching Publications.

Wray, A. (2002). *Formulaic language and the lexicon.* Cambridge University Press.

Yamagata, S., Nakata, T., & Rogers, J. (2022). Effects of distributed practice on the acquisition of verb-noun collocations. *Studies in Second Language Acquisition, 45*(2), 291-317.

Yorio, C. (1980). Conventionalized language forms and the development of communicative competence. *TESOL Quarterly, 14*(4), 433-442.

Zhang, X. (1993). *English collocations and their effect on the writing of native and non-native college freshmen* [Unpublished doctoral dissertation]. Indiana University of Pennsylvania.

Zhou, X. (2016). A corpus-based study on high frequency verb collocations in the case of "HAVE". *International Forum of Teaching and Studies, 12*(1), 42-50.

Zughoul, M. (1991). Lexical choice: Towards writing problematic word lists. *International Review of Applied Linguistics, 29,* 45-58.

Index

C

chronological, 30, 34, 38, 40, 41, 45-47, 54-57, 84, 88-90, 102, 104
colligation, 18, 21-23, 33, 38, 39, 57, 59, 64, 65, 85, 95
colligational, 23, 41, 58-65, 89, 95, 103
concgramming, 2-4, 20, 26, 32
concgram(s), 18-20, 32, 38, 42, 46, 54, 57, 62-68, 70, 71, 73, 78-80, 83-86, 89-92
congruency, 2, 5, 10, 11, 17, 18, 26, 31, 32, 34, 37, 38, 41, 42, 45, 69-73, 78-80, 82-86, 93, 96, 97, 102
constituent variation, 2, 18, 20
core idiom(s), 18, 42, 68, 69, 85, 92

D

dispersion, 30, 34, 38, 40, 41, 45-49, 51-57, 84, 88, 89, 102, 104

F

figurative(s), 17, 18, 42, 68, 69, 85, 88, 92, 95

L

literal(s), 9, 17, 18, 33, 42, 68-71, 85, 88, 92, 95, 96

M

MI, 11, 29, 30, 34, 40
mutual information, 11

O

ONCE(s), 18, 42, 68

P

positional variation, 2, 18, 19

S

semantic transparency, 2, 10, 11, 18, 28, 33, 34, 38, 42, 45, 68, 70, 85, 92, 102

www.ingramcontent.com/pod-product-compliance
Lightning Source LLC
Chambersburg PA
CBHW070336230426
43663CB00011B/2335